RECONCILIATION

A STUDY OF
BIBLICAL FAMILIES
IN CONFLICT

RECONCILIATION

A STUDY OF
BIBLICAL FAMILIES
IN CONFLICT

MICHAEL S. MOORE

COLLEGE PRESS
PUBLISHING COMPANY
Joplin, Missouri

LIBRARY OF CONGRESS CATALOG CARD NUMBER: 94-72126
INTERNATIONAL STANDARD BOOK NUMBER: 0-89900-684-1

TABLE OF CONTENTS

ACKNOWLEDGMENTS

This book began as a sermon series in the early 1980s. Colleagues at the Preston Road Center for Christian Education in Dallas, Texas provided a unique set of circumstances whereby the original idea could take firmer shape and deeper root. Rubel Shelly helped to shepherd the first primitive draft to the printed page. Tom Olbricht, Robert Oglesby, Charlotte Ryerson, Michael West, Jim Woodroof, Michael King, LaGard Smith, Allan McNicol, Steve Laube, Darrell Jodock, and Bill Love all criticized and encouraged me by reading different portions of the growing manuscript. Jim Bury loaned me his wonderfully critical eye on several occasions. Tom Parker was a constant source of encouragement.

In addition, several churches wrestled with these stories in their adult Bible classes over a period of approximately fifteen years. Many thanks to the Allentown Church of Christ in Whitehall, Pennsylvania, the Preston Road, Prestoncrest and Waterview Churches of Christ in Dallas, Texas, the Turnpike Church of Christ in Grand Prairie, Texas, and the Northwest and Tatum Boulevard Churches of Christ in Phoenix, Arizona.

Finally, I am especially grateful for the support of my family. To experience their daily love, patience, and support is a marvelous blessing I will never take for granted.

This book is dedicated to my sons by the covenant and younger brothers by the Spirit—Josh and Joe.

FOREWORD

We live in a time when family and personal crises pervade much of human existence. Television, films, and newspapers devote much space and programming to the exploration and delineation of complex and painful problems. Personal crises are the steady fare of talk shows and advice columns. Churchgoers are not immune. One can pick up on the pervasiveness of such crises by giving attention to church announcements, requests for prayers in sharing groups, demand for counseling, and concrete examples set out in sermons and classes. How are believers to address and respond to these accelerating concerns? Most frequently the response consists of conventional wisdom passed down in the churches and in families, or contemporary training and studies in psychology and counseling. Too infrequently are these matters addressed from the perspective of the Scriptures, and in our heritage, especially the Old Testament.

In a real sense Mike Moore has plowed new ground, at least in restorationist circles. He has dared suggest that the Old Testament supplies insight into the dilemmas facing contemporary Christians. Despite a common impression that the Old Testament is antiquated and no longer offers authoritative nourishment for the church of Jesus Christ, New Testament writers claim otherwise. Paul wrote the believers in Rome: "For whatever was written in former days was written for our instruction, so that by steadfastness and by the encouragement of scriptures we might have hope" (Romans 15:4). With additional specificity the same sentiment is expressed in 2 Timothy. "All scripture is inspired by God and is useful for teaching, for reproof, for correction, and for training in righteousness, so that everyone who belongs to God may be proficient, equipped for every good work" (2 Timothy 3:16). In both cases the documents envisioned are the Old Testament. Specifically Paul assumed that the Old Testament addresses life's problems from the perspective of the God who is the Father of our Lord Jesus Christ. It does not provide the parameters for church approaches and structure, but it is still the very word of God in personal matters.

One need not read long in this book before becoming palpably aware that Mike Moore is eminently qualified to narrate specific personal crises, and relate these to similar dilemmas of persons in the Old Testament. He sets forth dramatic and concrete incidents because of his many years of astute observation as a ministering servant among the Lord's people. It does not take long for the reader to become immersed in the situations set out, or to think of similar incidents in her own life or that of fellow believers. Furthermore, Mike is excellently prepared through graduate education in the Old Testament so as to have a vivid and accurate sense of the circumstances disclosed in the Old Testament. He presents these ancient persons in such a manner that they become alive and seem fully parallel with contemporary individuals.

I am persuaded that what Mike has achieved in this book is Biblical interpretation or hermeneutics at its best. In order to understand a Biblical text one must explore the context. This Mike has done. Then in order to utilize that text so that it may have bearing upon a contemporary situation, one must ascertain how God spoke to the ancient crisis and in turn how he addresses a similar situation today. Mike accomplishes this goal vigorously and with the expertise of an Old Testament scholar.

One may not always agree with Mike's interpretation or application, but neither may be lightly brushed aside, since Mike has thought in depth about both the text and the application. In fact, because Mike has not carried out an extended application, room remains for the reader to explore the rest of the text and application in additional directions. Mike encourages the reader to do so by asking questions he himself has not answered. Perhaps the greatest value of this book is that it is suggestive rather than definitive.

I applaud Mike's inimitable efforts to bring the very word of God to bear upon the problems that trouble us so deeply in these days.

Thomas H. Olbricht
Pepperdine University

INTRODUCTION

Mark Twain tells the story of a dinner party where the host prattles on endlessly about the accomplishments of his ancestors.

"He took us about his drawing room, showing us the pictures. Finally, he stopped before a rude and ancient engraving. It was a picture of the court that tried Charles I. There was a pyramid of judges in Puritan slouch hats, and below them three bareheaded secretaries seated at a table. He put his finger upon one of the three and said, 'An ancestor of mine.'"

Without batting an eye, Twain pointed to one of the *judges* seated above the secretaries in the engraving, and said in a voice loud enough for everyone to hear,

"Ancestor of *mine*. But it is a small matter. I have others."[1]

Ouch! Truly no one knows how to skewer human pretentiousness on the sword of sarcasm like Mark Twain.

Near the end of his life, however, a chastened, more tempered Twain found himself reflecting on this incident. At the time, it seemed like the right thing to do. Indeed, Twain spent his whole life looking for opportunities to poke fun at human pretentiousness. Later, however, he questioned the motives behind his behavior.

Searching his soul, he came to an important realization. He realized that he and this man had something very basic in common. Both liked to highlight the accomplishments of their ancestors—and ignore the flaws. Reflecting further, he wondered whether this habit might not be ingrained in *all* human beings. How many of us, he wondered, tend to read our histories through rose-colored glasses?

"It was not noble in me to do it (i. e., embarrass this man in front of his friends). I have always regretted it since . . . This has not had a good effect on me, for it has made me vain, and that is a fault."[2]

A HOLISTIC VIEW OF HISTORY

Luke addresses the same human tendency in the book of Acts.

Stephen's sermon in Acts 7:2-53 is a marvelous piece of work. From a literary perspective, this speech creates a transitional bridge between the story of the Jerusalem church in Acts 1-6 and the powerful explosion of Christianity into Samaria and points north in chapters 7-28.[3] From a theological perspective, Acts 7 challenges us to read Scripture honestly, courageously, and prophetically.[4]

The key word here is the term *father* (and its derivative, *patriarch*). This term appears no less than twenty times in this speech, or approximately every 2.5 verses. The first fifteen of these appearances come in the opening historical résumé. The last five signal two subtle, yet important shifts in perspective. The first comes when the historical narrative about the fathers shifts in verse 39 to a triad of statements beginning *"our* fathers."

The second comes in verse 51, when Stephen launches a pair of sharp, blistering indictments against *"your* fathers."

Thus there are three recognizable stages in this speech. Third person narrative changes to first person cohortative, then to second person indictment. Like any good sermon, this one builds suspense by means of a well-crafted structure. And like any good sermon, the goal of this one is to highlight and proclaim a powerful biblical theology.

From opening address ("Brothers and *fathers"*) to concluding rebuke ("Which of the prophets did not your *fathers* persecute?"), Stephen leads his audience to a climactic point of decision. He challenges them to rethink their history. He asks them to grapple honestly with the tension in their history between *patriarchy* and *paternalism.* He demands that they recognize this tension for what it is—a common theme flowing through the very center of their national consciousness.

On the one hand, his heart swells with pride at Abraham's faith, at the courageous persistence of the fathers who suffered through centuries of Egyptian oppression, at the resolve of Moses' father to preserve his son from Pharaoh's butchers. (See Acts 7:2, 19, 20.) On the other hand, he recoils in shame and embarrassment at the petty jealousy in Joseph's brothers, the sectarian, parochial spirit in

Moses' detractors, the self-righteous bigotry in all those fathers who murdered the prophets, including the Righteous One himself, Jesus of Nazareth. (See Acts 7:9, 39, 52.)

Stephen's audience *formally* claims to revere this history. Piety and reverence for "the fathers" is an important part of Palestinian culture. But this is as far as it goes. Like Twain, Stephen truly admires his fathers, and wants to hold them up as exemplary models. Yet he also knows that preaching the *truth* about them is difficult, given the tradition with which he has to work, the audience to whom he has to speak, and the rose-colored pretentions behind which that audience likes to live.

So how should he read their history? Critically? or selectively? Honestly? or blindly? Should he engage in the sort of biased, embellished "history" one finds in so many of his contemporaries?[5] Or like Jesus, should he fearlessly proclaim the *whole* truth about their fathers, regardless of the consequences?[6]

We all know what he decided to do. And we all know how much it cost him. Amazingly, Stephen's audience stoned him to death *for reading their history holistically*. This fact ought to sober us considerably. It ought to make us ask whether audiences today, particularly religious audiences, still resist the whole truth about their pasts.

Do we build up traditions around our ancestors, too?

A CONTEMPORARY EXAMPLE

This question came home to me a few years ago when a colleague of mine invited me to present a chapter in this book to his Sunday morning adult Bible class. Grateful for the opportunity, I attempted to read Scripture to my audience the way Stephen did. I approached the great heroes of the Old Testament with deep respect, but as real human beings. I discussed the struggle in Esther as she wrestled with the decision whether to help her people. I asked them to feel something of Abraham's pain as he decided whether to lie to Pharaoh about his true relationship to Sarah. I focused their attention on Joseph's decision to keep his identity a secret from his brothers until the time was right and he could no longer hold back his love.

It didn't go over very well. Things got quieter and quieter until finally a lady on the back row, a veteran Sunday School teacher, raised her hand and blurted out:

"I can't believe anyone would say something like that about Esther! How dare you imply that Abraham was a liar! How dare you suggest that Joseph might not have revealed himself to his brothers!"

Others agreed with her so strenuously, I found myself wondering whether I'd shown up at the right address that day. Is this a *Christian* church?

Finally, things calmed down long enough for me to ask her to show me the error of my way. But she was not interested in reading these stories holistically. She was too busy trying to save Esther from contamination.

"You've got it all wrong because you fail to understand that these people aren't really like us. They have a special measure of the Holy Spirit that we will never have. These people are our heroes, our role models. *That's* why they're in the Bible."

That's when it finally hit me. Her heroes are not human. They no longer sin. Indeed, they cannot sin. No wonder she was angry. To her, I was not simply talking about a "new" way to read Scripture. I was attacking her favorite goddess. I was challenging some of her most cherished beliefs about the Bible. The glasses through which she read the Bible were so thick, so rose-colored, so totally out of touch with historical truth, the only "argument" she had left to justify her position was pure emotionalism.

Later I thanked my colleague for the experience because it so clearly revealed to me the depth of our dilemma. I began to see more clearly than ever what Stephen was trying to do. Stephen was trying to lead a complacent religious audience back to the *whole* truth about their history. He understood that when human heroes become gods, no one can identify with them any longer. I began to see that those who read Scripture this way fall into the same trap that ensnared Jerusalem's leaders.

I would not go so far as to say that a holistic historical approach to Scripture is dead today, but I would say it's in serious trouble. The more we resist it, the more we see a variety of shallow substitutes usurping its place. Sadly, this is precisely what is going on in many adult classes today as "Bible study." We need to be clear about this danger. Conflict resolution, the subject of this book, is an activity for real people in the real world who clearly understand what evil is and who God is.

No discussion of it will ever go over very well with people who read the Bible through rose-colored glasses.[7]

INTERPRETING SCRIPTURE

Gary Collier tells the story of a minister who once told him:

"People in my church are so illiterate about the Bible, I change things from it all the time and they never know the difference!"[8]

Gary calls the Bible *The Forgotten Treasure*, arguing convincingly that Jesus never read Scripture the way many do today. Jesus read Scripture the way it's supposed to be read. Jesus saw Scripture as a window into the very heart of God, a message from the Holy One to convict us of sin, a "wake-up call" from the Father to wean us away from our persistently adolescent denial of reality.

For Jesus, Scripture is a beacon of hope pointing us aloft toward a glorious future.

This is the way we need to read Scripture, too, if we want to learn what God has to say about reconciliation or any other cardinal biblical doctrine. If we truly want to discover the *truth*, then we will have to train ourselves to read Scripture the way the prophets do. We will have to take the time to excavate the text instead of inter it. Only then can we begin to learn the principles of conflict resolution buried deep within its marvelous pages.

This needs to be underlined today because biblical interpretation (*hermeneutics*) is undergoing a period of serious reexamination, especially among Christians who feel the Bible to be ultimately authoritative in matters of faith and practice.[9] No responsible student of the text can ignore this climate. Thus, we, too, need to pause at the outset of this study and lay out our own hermeneutical presuppositions.

First, I believe that the healing power of the Word of God, which I define as the incarnate, resurrected person of Jesus of Nazareth operating through the sanctifying ministry of the Holy Spirit, is the "therapy" God graciously provides and people genuinely need.[10]

Since Scripture is the primary, normative conduit for this Word, our canons must be broad enough to let the Word speak in all its fullness. To avail ourselves of the whole counsel of God, the Church needs to listen to Scripture carefully in its 66-book entirety. Only then will we have a chance of becoming, in Paul's words, "ministers of reconciliation" (2 Cor. 5:18).[11]

Second, I believe that the best way to become an expert in conflict resolution is first to become a minister of reconciliation. Apart from genuine Christian ministry, I do not believe we will ever find the holistic, enduring answers we need to the conflicts which persistently divide us. And apart from the animating power of Scripture, the various "ministries" which occupy so many today in the name of Christ cannot truly be called "Christian."[12] Shortcuts will always be attractive. What we *really* need, though, is to put down our self-help books, throw away our quick-and-easy seminar manuals, and refocus our attention on the depth and breadth of Scripture. Only then can we legitimately expect to rediscover the power of God to resolve our conflicts and heal our lives. The primary reason why conflict demoralizes so many families today, even Christian families, is because we are too much like Twain and his dinner host. Do we seriously believe we can go on reading the Bible through rose-colored glasses and *still* tap into the spiritual resources we need to resolve our conflicts?

Third, I believe that the social sciences (psychology, anthropology, and sociology) have been and can continue to be valuable tools for constructing and implementing a holistic ministry of reconciliation. Extremists disagree about this, and I believe they need to be challenged. I believe that the social sciences can not only help us to read the diverse cultures into which God has called us to proclaim the Word,[13] but they can also help us to read Scripture itself.[14] In spite of the abuses (and there are many), I firmly believe that the social sciences, captured by the Word, can and should play an ongoing role in a holistic ministry of reconciliation.

Of course, the presuppositions upon which they're based need to be monitored carefully. The reasons for this should be obvious, and have, at any rate, been discussed elsewhere in great detail.[15] It is enough here to reiterate that whenever a secularist ideology is allowed to set the agenda for ministry, Scripture is emptied of its power. With Paul, I too believe that authentic conflict resolution is impossible when Scripture is held captive to the "elemental spirits of the universe" (Col. 2:8).[16]

Both extremes need to be avoided. We should neither ignore the valid contributions the social sciences have to make, nor should we simply accept their presuppositions *carte blanche*, no questions asked.[17] The balanced position is the middle one. I believe we should allow the social sciences to speak, at least when it comes to responsible *diagnosis* of the human dilemma, yet we should never allow them to speak louder than Scripture, particularly when it comes to hammering out a *prognosis* to this dilemma.[18]

THE GOAL OF THIS BOOK

Mark Twain and his colleagues like to ridicule our dilemmas and satirize our failures, sometimes in the crudest possible way. Satire, however, is not ministry. Situation comedy brings no lasting relief to human pain.[19]

True, Christians enjoy a good laugh as much as anyone else. But we are not naive. We know what our mission is. God wants to use us in his Kingdom to bring hope to the world and the lonely individuals within it by leading each one back, piece by broken piece, to Himself. We know that the Creation is "good" (Gen. 1:31). Indeed, the Creation can be a place of astonishing beauty at times. Yet we also know that the Creation groans to be redeemed from the forces of evil which now hold it captive (Rom. 8:18-25 and Eph. 2:2).

Conflict is therefore a familiar word. We see conflict between spouses and long to see sacrificial love. We see conflict between siblings and long to see respect, or at least peace. We see conflict between nations and shudder before its terrifying destructiveness. We see conflict between Christians and ache in frustration over it, knowing full well that it breaks the Lord's heart, divides us from one another, and cripples our common witness (John 17:20-26). We even see conflict within ourselves as we agonize, with Paul, over the sin which so easily besets each one of us (Rom. 7:7-20).

The question is, what can we do about it? Where can we go for help? How can we learn, in the words of Jesus, to become better peacemakers in the Kingdom when Mondays often call us to live and work in a ruthless, selfish and abusive world? As believers in the power of Scripture, how can the time we spend in Bible study be utilized more effectively to deal with these conflicts?[20]

I believe that the Old Testament is a depository of stories deliberately and faithfully preserved to help us deal with this dilemma. Sadly, it has become inaccessible to many today. The problem, again, has to do with the way we read it. Too often the Old Testament is perceived as just that . . . *old*. And anything *old*, in our culture, is synonymous with "out-of-touch," "outdated" and "irrelevant."[21] This means that two-thirds of our Bibles, for all practical purposes, are becoming obsolete for many. Let's be honest. Is it not true that the Old Testament is becoming little more than an antiquated oddity, a strange, confusing document for many of us? Truth be told, don't many of us read our spiritual history, when we read it at all, the way Mark Twain read his?[22]

I think we need to rediscover the power now buried within the pages of the Old Testament. We need to find out how biblical families resolved *their* conflicts if we ever expect to begin the necessary, painful process of healing *ours*.

We need to do more than just recapture our ancient heritage.

We need to get on with the business of teaching it to our children and grandchildren.

This is the goal of the following book. I want not only to demystify and bring to life some of the most important episodes in our common spiritual history, I also want to learn from them how to become a better minister of reconciliation. To this end, each chapter breaks down into three basic parts: *exposition, illustration,* and *application.* Each begins with an illustrative story, then focuses on a concise exposition of a biblical story, then transitions back to a contemporary application of this biblical story.[23] Questions and notes are provided at the end of each chapter for those who want to study in more depth. It goes without saying that all names and events in this book are fictitious, though each episode is inspired by an actual incident from my own experience.

Reflecting the diversity of the human family, each of the biblical families discussed below is caught up in a different kind of conflict. Hannah struggles over what to do about the barrenness in her womb. Jonathan wrestles with his father over leadership style. Miriam challenges her brother about the nature and limits of prophetic authority. Joseph inherits a sibling conflict going all the way back to the rivalry between Jacob-Esau and Isaac-Ishmael. Abigail falls into a violent dispute between two stubborn men and masterfully nips it in the bud before it has a chance to escalate.

In short, these families face the same conflicts we do. These are not simply children's stories, though children love them dearly. Nor are they preserved to entertain and amuse us, though they've held people spellbound for millennia.

Each is rather a powerful weapon in the arsenal of the Holy Spirit. One of them speaks directly to the conflict in your life.

QUESTIONS FOR DISCUSSION

(1) What was Mark Twain's problem?
(2) What was the point of Stephen's speech?
(3) What was the Sunday School teacher's problem?
(4) What are the three basic presuppositions undergirding the approach to Scripture adopted in this book?
(5) What is the goal of this book?

ENDNOTES

[1]Charles Neider, ed., *The Autobiography of Mark Twain* (New York: Harper and Row, 1959) pp.16-17.

[2]*Ibid.*, p. 17.

[3]Gerhard Krodel, *Acts* (Proclamation Commentaries; Philadelphia: Fortress, 1981) p. 31.

[4]Hans Conzelmann, *Acts of the Apostles* (Hermeneia; Philadelphia: Fortress, 1987) pp. 57-58.

[5]See, for example, *The Lives of the Prophets* in James Charlesworth, ed., *The Old Testament Pseudepigrapha*, vol. 2 (Garden City, NY: Doubleday, 1985) pp. 385-389.

[6]In John 8:44, Jesus boldly says to the scribes and the Pharisees, "You are of your father, the devil."

[7]Douglas John Hall says it well: "Whoever tries to read the Bible without taking serious note of the 'calamitous' nature of the history to which it bears witness, and whoever makes of it a success story with predictable, Horatio Alger-type motifs will have misunderstood the Bible in a truly fundamental way"; *God and Human Suffering: An Exercise in the Theology of the Cross* (Minneapolis: Augsburg, 1986) p. 32.

[8]Gary Collier, *The Forgotten Treasure: Reading the Bible Like Jesus* (West Monroe, LA: Howard Publishing, 1993) p. 3.

[9]Paul Pollard carefully reviews the problems and pitfalls in his "Recent Trends in Biblical Interpretation," *Restoration Quarterly* 34 (1992) pp. 65-81.

[10]Robert C. Roberts puts it this way: "This Word is the background of all deepest and truest healing of persons . . . the "-logy" of the true psychology; it is the Word of the soul, which must be brought to the fore and asserted once again, and thought through and placed in perspicuous comparison with the other psychologies that sound daily in our ears and bid to form us in their image"; *Taking the Word to Heart: Self and Other in an Age of Therapies* (Grand Rapids: Eerdmans, 1993) pp. xi-xii. Notice I do not say, with John MacArthur and others, that *the Bible* is all the therapy we need. Tim Stafford explores the implications of MacArthur's extremism in "The Therapeutic Revolution: How Christian Counseling is Changing the Church," *Christianity Today* 37, 6 (May 17, 1993) pp. 24-32.

[11]It is vitally important to remember, with Karl Barth, that "Scripture is in the hands but not in the power of the Church"; *Church Dogmatics* I/2,

p. 682, cited in Donald G. Bloesch, *Essentials of Evangelical Theology*, Vol. I: *God, Authority, and Salvation* (San Francisco: Harper and Row, 1978) p. 60.

[12]Haddon Robinson says much the same thing: "Sometimes you hear folks talk about *my ministry*. Using these two words together is wretched spiritual grammar. God calls us to no service or ministry that we do by ourselves"; "Proverbial Pests: The Wisdom of Little Things," *Christianity Today* 36, 5 (April 27, 1992) p. 28.

[13]Forty years ago Harold Lindsell said, "the best missionaries have been good anthropologists"; *Missionary Principles and Practices* (New York: Fleming H. Revell, 1955) p. 278.

[14]See Norman K. Gottwald, *The Hebrew Bible: A Socio-Literary Introduction* (Philadelphia: Fortress, 1985) pp. 20-31.

[15]See, for example, Peter L. Berger, "Different Gospels: The Social Sources of Apostasy," in Richard John Neuhaus, ed., *American Apostasy: The Triumph of "Other" Gospels* (Grand Rapids: Eerdmans, 1982) pp. 1-14.

[16]This is the thrust of Roberts, *Taking the Word to Heart*, who goes beyond criticism of "secular" psychology to formulating truly Christian psychology (pp. 151-308).

[17]Not everyone agrees with this synthesis. My colleague Michael Weed, for example, takes a rather dim view of the social sciences; "Secularized Religion in American Culture," in C. L. Allen, R. T. Hughes and M. R. Weed, *The Worldly Church: A Call for Biblical Renewal*, 2nd ed. (Abilene: Abilene Christian University, 1991) pp. 11-24. On the other hand, populist gurus like Melody Beattie have little real use for Scripture; *Codependent No More* (New York: Harper and Row, 1987).

[18]The problem comes to a head whenever we try to define our terms. Take the term *codependence*, for example. Can this word still be used today to describe a legitimate problem? Or is it too laden with secularist baggage to be useful to the Church? Melody Beattie uses the term loosely to describe over 200 types of "addiction," everything from alcoholism to incest, all within an omni-spiritual, pseudo-Christian worldview. Anne Wilson Schaef strongly reacts: "Recovery from the disease of co-dependence is impossible without recognizing and working with spiritual issues. Mental health practitioners do not know how to do that. In fact, in mental health circles, there is great suspicion of the spiritual. The mental health field has confused spirituality and religion and does not know how to deal with either"; *Codependence: Misunderstood, Mistreated* (San Francisco:

Harper and Row, 1986) p. 92. In my view, neither Beattie nor Schaef offer much to Christian ministers of reconciliation because neither one of their approaches is even close to being anchored in a biblical theology. In addition, Stan J. Katz and Aimee E. Liu attack the whole codependency movement as *psychologically* unhealthy; *The Codependency Conspiracy* (New York: Warner Books, 1991).

[19]Neil Postman, *Amusing Ourselves to Death: Public Discourse in the Age of Entertainment* (New York: Viking, 1985).

[20]This is the question raised by Reinhold Niebuhr in much of his work; for example, *The Nature and Destiny of Man* (New York: Scribner's, 1951).

[21]Like Twain, Thomas Oden also uses satire—to ridicule those who equate "new" with "good" and "old" with "bad." See Oden's classic *After Modernity . . . What?* (Grand Rapids: Zondervan, 1990) p. 42.

[22]James D. Smart, *The Strange Silence of the Bible in the Church* (Philadelphia: Westminster, 1970); Collier, *The Forgotten Treasure*.

[23]Bill Love emphasizes the value of story as an interpretive category in *The Core Gospel: On Restoring the Crux of the Matter* (Abilene: Abilene Christian University, 1992) pp. 101-104.

ABIGAIL'S DILEMMA

(1 SAMUEL 25:2-42)

"That's the stupidest play I've ever seen! I've seen *morons* who can play better than you! Why do you always do this to me? I'm sick and tired of your . . . !"

"*Stop it!*" my breaking voice said. I had heard enough. All four of us just stared at each other, suddenly sprayed with tension, acutely aware of the abrupt shift in the evening's mood.

To do something, *anything*, I asked Jim to go outside with me for a walk. Pushing back our chairs from the table, I will never forget the wild, burning glare he shot at me. This man was a seething volcano ready to erupt.

It was supposed to be a friendly game of *Scrabble*. Jim and Sarah were a young couple new to our community. We were a young minister and his wife inviting them over for Friday night supper. After dessert we got out the game, one of our favorites, and began to play. Someone suggested we play couple against couple. Nobody objected, so that's what we did. Everyone seemed to be having a good time. Anyone who has ever played *Scrabble* into the wee hours of the evening knows what I mean. Things can get silly. Inventing weird, strange words can be half the fun.

Not for Jim. Shivering together in the winter cold, I asked him what in the world could have triggered a tantrum like the one he had just thrown in my dining room. How could he speak to his wife so harshly? How could he possibly justify such dehumanizing language?

Sheepishly, apologetically, he said,

"I'm under a lot of stress right now. I don't know the area yet, and my boss expects me to do the impossible. The moving company lost some of our things, and our kids don't like their new school. We miss our friends back home terribly. I really didn't mean what I just said."

He seemed genuinely sorry for causing a scene.

I felt genuinely sorry for him.

Assuming he was ready to go in and apologize to his wife, I led him back into the house. At first, neither of them even looked at each other. No one wanted to make the first move. My wife had that "What's going on?" look in her eyes. Steeling myself for the possibility of entering into a crisis counseling experience with a couple I really didn't know, I had no idea what was going to happen next.

Then, like a switch turning on, Sarah began to talk and act as if nothing had happened. She asked if she could help with the dishes. She asked about the neighborhood where we lived. She asked about the children's Bible classes at church. With every word forcing its way from her mouth I felt more and more perplexed. She even made an effort to include Jim in the conversation, speaking to her husband in careful, measured tones:

"Jim, where was that place? What was the name of that lady, you know, Mrs., uh, what was her name? Jim, dear, could you wake up the children while I help clean up? We'll have to have *them* over some time, won't we honey?"

It was just so . . . odd. Coming on the heels of the evening's earlier eruption, the polite normalcy in her voice seemed absurdly out of place.

She talked to her husband the way a patient mother speaks to a pouting child. Yet not once did Jim make even the slightest effort to respond, much less initiate an apology. The pattern was well-established. She chatted politely to fill up the silence while he sat scowling in a corner, grunting only when spoken to. Slowly, unbidden, a question began swimming its way to the surface of my consciousness: "How long has *this* been going on?"

Sadly, what we had witnessed that evening was painfully routine. Volcanic Jim habitually blew up at mild-mannered Sarah, once even before the whole congregation during a volleyball game. Each time it happened, Sarah patiently cleaned up the mess. To a few close friends, she dared to grieve. She confessed she didn't know how much longer she could hold on. She believed in the institution of marriage. The very thought of divorce violated every value she held dear. Yet the reality of life with Jim was taking its toll. Her "love bank," to use Willard Harley's helpful phrase, was close to empty.[1] Too many withdrawals. Not enough deposits.

Valiantly she hung on, hoping that somehow, someday Jim would eventually grow up. That day never came. Soon after they moved away we were saddened, but not surprised to hear of their divorce. The news came to us on the back of a Christmas card, the front of which ironically proclaimed:

"PEACE ON EARTH!
GOOD WILL TOWARD MEN!"

THE STORY

Abigail's ministry of reconciliation is a polished jewel set in the midst of a larger setting. Like most gems, it can best be appreciated by viewing it against its broader historical and literary context.

When David kills Goliath, he has no idea how much this one act of courage is going to intimidate Saul. He just wants to serve God. Saul, however, is an insecure man who cannot tolerate success in others, especially in those he considers his subordinates. So David has to go underground to escape his anger.

A motley crew of malcontents soon surfaces in his wake. The core of this group consists of men who hate Saul—his bureaucracy in Gibeon, his reign of terror, his entire leadership style. Deeply in debt and desperate for a leader to champion their cause, they turn to David. Running for their lives, they come to a small village called Nob. Here David approaches a small religious sanctuary for food and shelter, his guerrilla band now swollen to about four hundred men. Incredibly, Saul massacres the entire village in a reckless attempt to kill him. Like other tyrants, he prefers a shotgun to a revolver. He commits genocide. (Cf. Exod. 1:15-22 and Matt. 2:16-18.) Shamelessly he exterminates no less than eighty-five priests of Yahweh plus an unspecified number of men, women and children. From any perspective, this is a vicious act by a paranoid tyrant. That it goes largely unpunished shows how powerful Saul has become. It also says something about why so many are beginning to turn to David for alternative leadership.

News of the massacre quickly spreads. After Nob, the village of Keilah will have nothing to do with David, even though he previously saved it from Philistine marauders. Residents of the wilderness of Ziph are so afraid of his presence they report him to Saul like frightened puppies, yelping and cowering before the junkyard dog.

David thus finds himself in a precarious position. Straddled with the responsibility of feeding a small army, he finds it increasingly difficult to make ends meet. The stress begins to get to him. He becomes desperate—desperate enough to turn to a rather time-honored, yet questionable means of fundraising. Like Robin Hood in medieval England or mujahedin in modern Afghanistan, David goes into the shady business of "protecting" the property of wealthy landowners. To cite a line made famous by Mario Puzo, David makes landowners "offers they can't refuse."[2]

Nabal is one of those landowners.

From the narrator's perspective there doesn't seem to be anything really wrong with this "business." At least this is the impression that is left. From Nabal's perspective, however, there's a lot wrong with it! Understandably, he wants no part of David or his offer of "protection."

But this is not a story about Nabal. This is a story about David, a memorable chronicle about Israel's most resourceful king. Ultimately it's designed to explain how David managed to consolidate power in the South by means of political marriage to a beautiful southern woman, Abigail. To appreciate it fully, it needs to be read alongside the story of consolidation in the North in 2 Samuel 5:1-5.

Perspective is everything. Rather than offer us a preachy essay on the propriety of David's ethics, the narrator instead pens a hilarious satire on Nabal's stupidity. The depth of this stupidity comes to us from three different angles: *directly* by the narrator, *indirectly* through a speech by Nabal's foreman, and *summarily* through a speech by Abigail.

NABAL THE "FOOL"

The narrator leads the charge by introducing Nabal to us as a "difficult" man, a man "evil of actions." The first of these terms is found elsewhere in descriptions of Joab (2 Sam. 3:39), Saul (1 Sam. 20:10), and Rehoboam (1 Kings 12:13), unsavory characters all. The second occurs in biblical passages where Israel is stiff-necked and impenitent, especially in the prophetic literature. Hosea, for example, warns of a time when Samaria's "evil actions" will be revealed for all the world to see. (Hosea 7:2. See also Judg. 2:19 and Jer. 11:18.)

Nabal's foreman then embellishes this description in a speech to Abigail containing two pointed contrasts. First, the foreman says that even though David's messengers are attempting to bless Nabal, Nabal's response is embarrassing. He "shrieks" at them. The original language here is vivid. The Hebrews describe a certain species of bird with a term that sounds something like "*eeet!*" This high-pitched, screeching sound is the sound that Nabal shouts at David's men. Like a vulture swooping down on a carcass, Nabal's way of resolving conflict is to scream and intimidate, not reflect and pray.

Second, this behavior goes on in spite of the fact that David's men are "very good" to Nabal and his servants. Thus, the foreman cannot understand why Nabal acts like a "son of Belial."[3] "Belial" is a particularly strong word, meaning "worthless." "Son of Belial" is Hebrew shorthand for a worthless ingrate, especially one opposed to the monarchy.[4]

The same epithet comes up again in Abigail's speech, when she tries to explain his behavior.

"Let not my lord regard this Belial-like man, Nabal. For he is just like his name. Nabal is his name, and folly is with him."[5]

ABIGAIL'S DILEMMA

In other words, Abigail faces a situation very much like that which faces mediators everywhere.[6] She has to resolve a dispute between two stubborn people. On the one hand is a man who thinks he can stand up to an army of four hundred by himself:

> Who is David? Who is the son of Jesse? There are many servants nowadays who are breaking away from their masters. Shall I take my bread and my water and my meat I have killed for my shearers, and give it to men who come from who knows where? (1 Sam. 25:10-11).

On the other is a man who thinks he has a divine right to "protect" people when they refuse to knuckle under and give him what he wants:

> Surely in vain have I guarded all that this fellow has in the wilderness, so that nothing was missed of all that belonged to him; and he has returned me evil for good! May God do so to David and more also if by morning I leave so much as one male of all who belong to him! (1 Sam. 25:21-22).

Both men are headstrong and pigheaded. This not only makes for a compelling story, it also provides Abigail a golden opportunity. Because the speeches just cited so clearly reveal for us the flaws in the main characters of this story, the temptation is great to discuss at length Nabal's self-centeredness or David's impetuosity. To go in this direction, however, would lead us away from our other main character, Abigail. Her role has been neglected, downplayed, or ignored in most readings of this text. This is regrettable, because this heroine has a great deal to teach us about conflict resolution.

Her immediate problem seems obvious: how to convince two angry, stubborn men just to listen to her. There's just no way she can bring genuine reconciliation between David and Nabal unless she first convinces them to sit down and listen to what she has to say. No doubt she knows from experience that Nabal won't listen, so she doesn't bother to go to him first. Instead, she goes directly to David.

Yet behind this story is an even broader context.

Hebrew narrators never tire of telling stories about "powerless" women who always get their way with powerful men, often by highly inventive means. The Canaanite widow Tamar triumphs over Judah, her father-in-law, even though Judah lies to her, has illicit sexual intercourse with her, and threatens her life (Gen. 38:1-26). Jael kills the Canaanite general Sisera after enticing him into her tent with an offer of shelter (Judg. 5:24-30). Esther is a reluctant queen who, after balking and hesitating, manipulates Haman the Agagite into hanging himself on his own gallows (Esth. 5:1-7:10).

Each one of these stories features a seemingly powerless heroine overcoming great odds in order to achieve what seem to be impossible goals. Tamar disguises herself, then forces Judah to account for his behavior publicly (Gen. 38:14). Esther creates an atmosphere of trust by inviting Haman to a series of royal dinner parties, then successfully accuses him of plotting genocide (Esth. 5:4). Judith plies Holofernes with alcohol until he collapses in a drunken stupor, then decapitates him (Judith 13:1-11, in the Apocrypha).

Similarly, Abigail arranges a kingly meal and brings it to David before his anger has a chance to build up a head of steam. Thus securing his attention, this mediator then takes three deliberate steps in order to defuse their conflict.

First, she assumes responsibility.

"Upon me alone, my lord, be the guilt" (1 Sam. 25:24).

In other words, she performs the most responsible adult action in the story. She takes responsibility for resolving this conflict. She doesn't run away or otherwise seek to evade this responsibility. Nor does she allow herself to get sucked up into the conflict by taking sides and pointing blame. She simply decides to stop it. Like Jesus on the Cross, pleading for God to forgive a mob, Abigail puts herself directly in harm's way. This is an astoundingly brave woman.

Second, she does something even more startling. She swears an oath in direct response to David's oath:

"As the Lord lives, and as your soul lives, seeing the Lord has restrained you from bloodguilt, and from taking vengeance with your own hand . . . " (1 Sam. 25:26).

Oaths are not a light matter in ancient Israel. As a matter of fact, ancient Near Eastern oaths and vows were powerful social contracts designed to bring down unalterable consequences on the heads of those who violated them. Once an oath was done there was no easy way to have one undone. Even rash oaths had to be kept (Lev. 5:1-6).[7]

By invoking Yahweh's name in an oath, Abigail deliberately and courageously places her life at risk. She does this in order to startle David into realizing how rash he has been in his own oath-taking. Abigail realizes that serious mediation of emotional disputes always involves an appropriate measure of risk.

Finally, after securing David's attention, she tries to reason with him regarding the implications of his planned assassination. Would not such a course of action render his leadership as wicked as

Saul's, the tyrant who slaughtered the innocents at Nob? By killing Nabal, would David not also be guilty of shedding innocent blood? Would he not be guilty of exacting vengeance which properly belongs to the Lord?

CONFLICT RESOLUTION

Conflict resolution is big business today. In the corporate business world, one consultant breaks it down into six basic areas:

(1) *External* conflicts related to competition, regulation or an adversarial takeover (David's "protection" of Nabal's land);

(2) *Management* conflicts stemming from leadership style, poor decision-making, or poor organizational structure (David's struggle to counter Saul, yet not become another Saul);

(3) *Strategic* conflicts involving uncertainty over an organization's overall direction and vision (David's struggle to come to grips with his rash oath-taking);

(4) *Operational* conflicts involving the day-to-day frictions of any corporate body (David's problems making ends meet for a growing army);

(5) *Interdepartmental* conflicts which occur when subdivisions of an organization battle over "turf" (Nabal's men trying to cooperate with David's men);

(6) *Value* conflicts where moral norms and basic worldviews collide (Abigail's brilliant speech persuading David not to turn into that which he hates).[8]

The conflict between David and Nabal easily shows signs of all six types. Not only does this raise our appreciation for the difficulty of Abigail's dilemma, it also underscores our amazement at her mediatorial skills. Most mediators have to juggle one, two, or three balls in the air at the same time. Abigail juggles six.

Category six, however, is where she really shines. The method she uses to help David think through his most basic values involves three elements: *responsibility, initiatory risk,* and *reason.* Attention to each of these elements is crucial if we truly want to understand and appreciate the biblical doctrine of reconciliation.

We live in an irresponsible age. Ambrose Bierce sarcastically defines "responsibility" as "a detachable burden easily shifted to the shoulders of God, Fate, Fortune, Luck or one's neighbor."[9]

When a person, family or business fails to take responsibility, the result is *chaos*. This chaos destroys families, communities, businesses, and churches. Commenting on this chaos in an important magazine article, Robert Hughes points to it as directly responsible for the "fraying of America."[10] Chuck Colson calls our age a new "dark age."[11]

What can be done about it? To the extent that we realize and practice a genuine ethic of responsibility, to that extent our families, communities, businesses and churches will succeed in doing what they're supposed to do. To the extent that we rediscover what Scott Peck calls "civility," the Christian ministers of reconciliation among us will help us begin to understand the glorious nature of Abigail's accomplishment.[12]

Abigail is a woman who dares to take responsibility for her own actions and those of her loved ones. She refuses to "pass the buck" onto someone else's shoulders. Abigail is an adult. But more than this, she is a person who understands how essential it is, particularly in situations of a delicate nature, to take a measured risk. She knows that conflict cannot be resolved until someone makes the first move to resolve it. Conflicts like the one between Nabal and David are moments of opportunity for people like Abigail.

Eduard Shevardnadze, a seasoned Soviet diplomat, claims in his autobiography that it is the unexpected grace, the unplanned kindness which often is the key to breaking stubborn deadlocks and providing breakthroughs. One such instance occurred during a round of arms talks between Shevardnadze and his counterpart, Secretary of State James Baker. Frustrated by the way things were going in their talks, Baker decided to invite Shevardnadze to visit his elderly mother in Texas on a whim. In response, Shevardnadze was so touched by the gesture, negotiations warmed up immediately between the two men and an arms agreement was soon reached. None of this could have happened had Baker not been willing, like Abigail, to take an initiatory risk.[13]

Finally, after David is softened up by Abigail's one-two punch of *responsibility* plus *risk*, the stage is set to try *reason*. Note her timing. Had she tried reason first, chances are her negotiations would have failed. Timing, in the matter of conflict resolution, is everything. Skilled negotiators know that a lot more can be accomplished over a dinner table than a battlefield. Realizing this, David eventually praises Abigail for her "discretion," a term often used in Scripture to describe someone unusually wise, as in the great wisdom psalm: "Teach me discretion and knowledge for I have trusted in your commandments" (Ps. 119:66) or the satirical proverb: "Like a gold ring in a swine's snout is a beautiful woman without discretion" (Prov. 10:22).

Now sufficiently softened up, David finally listens to her arguments and relents. Abigail's arguments are simply too sound, her methods too persuasive, her timing too impeccable. Like Judah with Tamar, David finally acknowledges the superior wisdom of a "powerless" woman whom God has mercifully placed in his life.[14]

The story concludes when Nabal drinks himself to death, David marries Abigail and everyone lives "happily ever after." Yet the "fairy tale" ending the narrator lets us see takes nothing away from the magnitude of Abigail's achievement. If anything, it heightens it. No mediator has any guarantee that *responsibility*, *risk* and *reason*, apart from another "r" word—*repentance*—will do anything to resolve conflict today.

But we can say that genuine reconciliation is usually impossible without them.

QUESTIONS FOR DISCUSSION

(1) Without naming names, do you know any Abigails today?
(2) Do you know any Nabals today? Describe.
(3) How would you describe Jim's problem?
(4) How well do you think Sarah handled it?
(5) Why is Nabal so negatively portrayed in this story?
(6) What steps does Abigail take to resolve the conflict between David and Nabal?
(7) Why do you think this story is preserved in Scripture?

ENDNOTES

[1]Willard F. Harley, Jr., *His Needs, Her Needs* (Old Tappan, NJ: Revell, 1986).

[2]Mario Puzo, *The Godfather* (New York: G. P. Putnam's Sons, 1969).

[3]This phrase is preserved intact in the King James Version.

[4]In later texts this term becomes a proper name for the Prince of Evil. Benedikt Otzen discusses it at length in the *Theological Dictionary of the Old Testament*, vol. 2 (Grand Rapids: Eerdmans, 1975) pp. 131-136.

[5]*Nabal* is one of several Hebrew words for "fool."

[6]For example, the "wise woman" of Tekoa in 2 Samuel 14:1-20. P. Kyle McCarter thinks that Abigail, for all practical purposes, is herself a "wise woman"; *2 Samuel* (Anchor Bible 9; Garden City, NY: Doubleday, 1984) p. 345. For further study, see M. S. Moore, "Wise Women or Wisdom Woman? A Biblical Study of Women's Roles," *Restoration Quarterly* 35 (1993) pp. 147-158.

[7]Jephthah takes an oath in Judges 11:30-40 which cannot be undone even though it results in the death of his daughter.

[8]John D. Arnold, *When the Sparks Fly: Resolving Conflicts in Your Organization* (New York: McGraw-Hill, 1993) p. 56.

[9]Ambrose Bierce, *The Devil's Dictionary*, cited in Robert C. Solomon and Kristine R. Hanson, *Above the Bottom Line: An Introduction to Business Ethics* (New York: Harcourt, Brace, Jovanovich, 1983) p. 207.

[10]Robert Hughes, "The Fraying of America," *Time* 139, 5 (Feb 3, 1992) pp. 44-49.

[11]Chuck Colson, *Against the Night: Living in the New Dark Ages* (Ann Arbor, MI: Servant Publications, 1989) pp. 9-13.

[12]M. Scott Peck, *A World Waiting to Be Born: Civility Rediscovered* (New York: Bantam, 1993) pp. 3-6.

[13]Eduard Shevardnadze, *The Future Belongs to Freedom* (translated by Catherine A. Fitzpatrick; New York: Free Press, 1991) p. 72.

[14]In Genesis 38:26 Judah says of Tamar, "She is more righteous than I."

ABRAHAM'S TEMPTATION

(GENESIS 12:1-22:18)

The room is so filled with smoke I can hardly breathe.

It hangs from the ceiling like a dirty smog, burning my eyes and throat, choking my lungs and making me cough.

Mel scans the crowd, spots his Dad, and begins to cut a path his way. Taking a deep breath, I plunge into his wake, wondering why so many recovering alcoholics turn to cigarettes instead of, say, chewing gum.

We have arrived late to the weekly *Alcoholics Anonymous* meeting at *United Steelworkers Union Hall #257*, and seats are scarce. Asked why the place is so crowded, Dad says it's the recent layoffs at "the Steel," the gigantic foundry which controls the economy of this Pennsylvania community like an aortic valve. When "the Steel" clogs up, so does everything else. Lately the Steel has been going through a series of economic heart attacks. Accustomed to running four smelters 24 hours a day, it now runs only one smelter 8 hours a day.

Cutbacks that severe always mean one thing. Layoffs. And layoffs always translate into something else. Shattered male egos. Hundreds of them. Thousands of them, their shattered, splintering shards littering the homes of our valley like broken glass in a parking lot. For most men, losing a job is traumatic.

Some survive it.

Others don't.

Some turn the trauma into greater opportunity.

Others turn to chemical anesthesia to escape the pain.

Intrigued by my curiosity, Mel's Dad shows me how to tell the newcomers from the regulars at an *AA* meeting. Newcomers look sheepish, nervous, embarrassed. Regulars look, well, determined.

Weary. A bit strung-out, perhaps. But determined nonetheless. Handshakes are firm. Eye contact is steady. Body language is open.

Mel is a newcomer.

Dad is a regular.

Almost everyone who knows Dad knows Mel. Dad has mentioned him often over the past two years. Everyone seems delighted, therefore, that Mel has decided to come to a meeting. They appreciate his courage. They know how difficult it is to reach out for help. Every one of them wrestles with the same demon he does. When several of the regulars come up to Mel and greet him, I am reminded of a crowd of Christians surrounding a newly baptized believer.

One by one they march up to the microphone. Their stories are tragic, powerful, heart-breaking. One middle-aged man in an expensive suit shares his fear of walking in front of an open tavern door. A demure older woman argues vehemently that hers is a battle against a rapacious monster. Not a sin, not a disease. A monster. A burly steelworker saunters up and spits out his story like chewed-up plugs of *Red Man* or *Bull Durham*. A bespectacled young widow begs us to help her get over the loss of her husband, the victim of an industrial accident at "the Steel."

It goes on like this for about an hour. No one hurries. No one looks at a watch. No one criticizes. No one rationalizes. Each speaker drinks deeply of the one substance they all know it's OK to drink. Unconditional acceptance. It's one of the most remarkable displays of *agape* love I have ever seen.

When I look up, Mel's dad is speaking. His bitterness is almost palpable. Though it's been two years since his layoff, the rage still emanates from him like a viral infection refusing to die. Matter-of-factly, he describes how this rage has destroyed his family. He regrets anniversaries forgotten and birthdays ignored. He laments public humiliations and uncounted embarrassments.

These are the same stories Mel has already told me in private. The time when Dad dislocated Mel's shoulder in a drunken rage. The time when Mom pulled out a kitchen knife to protect the boys from yet another vicious beating. The time when Dad slapped Mel full in the face, right in front of his girlfriend's parents. The time when Dad almost drowned in the pool at their wedding reception, he was so drunk.

How eerie it is to hear them again from another perspective. Unconsciously, the corner of my eye searches Mel's face for a response. Surely he can see what's going on. Is anything getting through? Is he totally calloused to his father's feelings? Dad has never publicly apologized like this before. Surely Mel must know that he's taking a risk by doing so now.

Yet the pain is deep. The defenses are well-anchored.

It is a pivotal moment. Dad speaks firmly. He looks directly at his son, not once, but several times. Other people begin to stare, carefully at first, then more obviously. Surely, I thought, Mel has to feel the emotion in those eyes. Intensely compassionate, they beg him to respond to their friend's inner pain. Would there ever be a better time for reconciliation? Would there ever be a more appropriate time for forgiveness? For all he knows, this could well be Dad's last, best attempt to say "I'm sorry."

Then it happens.

Without a word, Mel stands up, makes his way to the center aisle, and walks straight to the front of the room. Dad sees his silhouette through the smoke, gasps slightly, and stops talking, his voice trailing off in mid-sentence. Necks crane. People whisper. "What's going on?" "What's he going to do?" No one in the room has any idea of what's going to happen next.

Then I see it. You have to look for it, but it's there. It starts at the corner of his eyes, then spreads out over Mel's entire face. It radiates from his soul like a quiet Arizona sunset. It responds to all our stares with a power all its own, a new-found power, an eternal power.

It's that *look* Dad was talking about. That determined look.

Taking the microphone from his dad, Mel looks intently at the crowd and swallows hard. What's he going to say? After all the months of prayer, and counseling, and worship, and Bible study, what's he going to say? Is he finally going to admit his powerlessness? Is he finally going to deal with the sin which is ravaging his life?

The answer comes in seven short words:

"Hi. I'm Mel . . . and I'm an alcoholic."

THE STORY

The story of Abraham is a marvelous treasure. Its main character is one of Scripture's most revered heroes. Like other biblical stories, the story of Abraham generates a legend which grows to superhuman proportions. The Pharisees in Jesus' day proudly called themselves the "sons of Abraham," believing that the very name had saving power. (See Matt. 3:9 and John 8:39.)[1] Josephus regarded him as a sinless saint, a man who lived far above the mundane world of human temptation.[2] Triumphantly entering Mecca in the 7th century A.D., even Muhammad was astonished to discover that Abraham's image had been painted all over the sacred walls of the Ka'aba, Islam's holiest shrine. One of his first official acts was to have the walls of the Ka'aba scraped clean.[3]

The purpose of this chapter is to do something similar—scrape the rose-colored image of Abraham off *our* walls, the walls of our minds. Hopefully we will be able to replace it with a more holistic one. Abraham was not a god. Abraham was a man. A great man, a faithful man, but just a man nonetheless. The power of his example is not to be found in what he does for God. The power of his example is to be found in what God does through him.

The saga of his life opens on the world of a tribal chieftain struggling to survive a harsh environment. His moral code is tribal, his religion patriarchal, his economy agrarian, and his politics isolationist. The needs of his tribe take precedence over everything else in his life. This is the basis of his entire moral code.[4] The line he draws between truth and falsehood is based totally on a tribal type of morality.

Thus, like most tribal moralities, it tends to blur badly when Abraham has to interact with someone outside his own tribe.

Take Pharaoh, for example. Assuming that Sarah is unmarried, Pharaoh absorbs her into his harem (Gen. 12:10-20).[5] From an urban Egyptian perspective, there's nothing wrong with this behavior. But not from Abraham's perspective. In addition to being his sister, Sarah is also Abraham's wife, a tiny detail Abraham conveniently fails to mention to his host (Gen. 20:12). Abraham seems to withhold this truth because he does not want to endanger the parochial needs of his tribe. He doesn't overtly lie. He simply withholds the truth. He hides behind a tribal technicality.

To call him a liar doesn't really sound fair, but what is he, if not a liar? At the very least, Abraham is a man who lacks moral integrity.[6]

But in addition to this, he's faithless, too. Just look at the scene where he laughs at God (Gen. 17:17).[7] God promises him a son through Sarah and instead of trusting God, Abraham laughs at God. He can't believe it. Sarah is barren and old, too old to bear children by natural means. So Abraham assumes that she can't have children by *any* means, even supernatural means. Besides, Hagar has already given him Ishmael, and Abraham has already given Ishmael the rights and privileges of the firstborn son. Why rock the boat now? Why complicate Ishmael's inheritance?

The whole idea sounds preposterous.

But Abraham does more than just laugh. He tries to torpedo the idea altogether. He proposes that God retract his original idea and replace it with a more "realistic" one. He does what all unbelievers do, sooner or later. He tries to second-guess God. "Why not make Ishmael the child of promise? Why not allow him to be the conduit of your eternal blessings?"

"Oh that Ishmael might live in your sight!" (Gen. 17:18).

These are not minor flaws. Difficult as it sounds, particularly if we've had Abraham's positive traits pounded into our heads since childhood, Abraham (surprise!) is a sinner. He's a human being, just like you and me.

ABRAHAM AND GOD

Our God is very wise. (Read Ps. 139:1-18.) He knows us better than we know ourselves. Like a father fawning over his children, he persistently reaches out to us, even though we are stubborn and obstinate (Hosea 11:1-9). He cuts a blood covenant with us because he loves us—purely, genuinely and unconditionally. (See Deut. 7:6-11, Jer. 31:31-34, and Matt. 26:26-29.) He personifies this love in Jesus of Nazareth (John 15:12-17). He sanctifies it through the Holy Spirit (Eph. 1:13). He extends this covenant not just to the spiritually elite, but to all who trust in him (Matt. 8:11). He promises us that we will never be tested beyond that which we can reasonably endure (1 Cor. 10:6-13).

But he will test us. Often we conveniently forget to notice this side of God's being, especially when we focus only on his love to the neglect of his *holiness*. In a culture like ours, the temptation is great to forget that "Yahweh of the armies is his name. The Holy One of Israel is your redeemer" (Isa. 54:5).[8]

That's why when we lose our theological balance (and we often do), God becomes more and more difficult to understand, especially for our children. Texts like the one before us become impossible to comprehend, much less explain. Apart from a holistic view of the biblical God, who can explain why a good God would command Abraham to kill Isaac? Assuming that God is *only* a God of love, or grace, or tolerance leads us to utter astonishment before texts like this.[9]

Divine actions like this raise up our deepest, darkest fears about God, fears we would prefer to leave buried in our subconscious minds, not trot out in the middle of Sunday morning Bible class. Let's face it. We don't like to discuss this side of God. Often, in fact, someone nervously suggests at this point that we all turn to the New Testament, read something reassuring about the "faith of Abraham," and go home.[10]

Others deal with the tension by suggesting that the God of the Old Testament and the God of the New Testament must somehow be different Gods. Surely, the argument goes, the God and Father of our Lord Jesus Christ would never do what Abraham's God does. But this is desperately naive, what R. C. Sproul calls an "exegesis of despair."[11] Is there really a difference between Abraham's God and Jesus' Father? Contrast and compare. Jesus' God allowed *him* to be killed, did he not, while Abraham's God saved Isaac. Jesus' God stood silent while a howling mob mocked, scourged and crucified *his only Son*, right? Are we to conclude from this sort of comparison that Jesus' God is "kinder" than Abraham's God?

Temptations to mistreat this text come at us from many directions. We can rationalize it, dichotomize it, or simply ignore it if we so choose, but it won't go away. Serious students resist such temptations. Serious students of the Word know that unless we find out why God tests Abraham, we will probably continue to experience difficulty understanding and explaining to a "victims' rights" culture why God continues to test us.[12]

Abraham is not *born* a man of faith. He *becomes* a man of faith. Like most of us, it takes him a long time to develop his faith in God. He has to hurdle several obstacles first, resolve several internal and external conflicts.

Perhaps we need to back up, then, and take a closer look at *how* this all occurs.

ABRAHAM AS HUSBAND

Victor Kassel predicts that since women outlive men by approximately five to fifteen years, women will continue to outnumber men in our "graying" society for some time to come. Therefore, he suggests, men over sixty should be encouraged to take more than one wife. This would solve several problems now plaguing the elderly: loneliness, depression, poor diet, frequent illness, poor grooming, sexual frustration, and even the problem of health insurance (since it's easier to obtain for a group than for a couple!).[13]

Well, Abraham was over sixty when he took Hagar into his tent and look what happened to him! Hagar may have solved some of his problems, but like so many other marriages in Scripture involving rival wives, she brought a slew of problems with her, too. Obviously we cannot hold Abraham to the same monogamous standards that we enjoy, but we can, within the context of his own polygamy, ask some pointed questions about his faithfulness as a husband.

First, as has already been pointed out, Abraham unashamedly pushes Sarah into embarrassing moral dilemmas on at least two separate occasions. (See Gen. 12:10-20 and 20:1-18.) To be absorbed into another man's harem, particularly that of a foreigner, is degrading. Harem life is never a woman's first choice in Scripture. No woman wants to be treated like chattel, yet this is precisely how Abraham treats Sarah.[14]

The rabbis knew this. Trying to explain his behavior, they engaged in some rather creative exegesis to "protect his honor." They argued that the verb "to take" in the biblical phrase "she was *taken* into Pharaoh's palace" actually means "she was *elevated* into Pharaoh's palace" (Gen. 12:15).[15] It doesn't take a rocket scientist

to realize, however, that this is simply one more attempt to rationalize away a character flaw. No human being deserves to be treated
like negotiable property. Period. When Abraham engages in this
practice, he unavoidably strains his relationship with his wife, and
this comes back to haunt him later.

Hagar's entrance into Abraham's tent thus complicates an
already tenuous situation. Sensing this tenuousness, Hagar boldly
decides to treat Sarah with "contempt" after Ishmael is born.
Sarah's status has the potential of falling into real jeopardy because
fertile women are always paid more deference than infertile women
in the ancient Near East. Everyone in this story knows that.

Thus Sarah begins to fear Hagar, and this fear is not unfounded.
An unmistakable feeling of panic invades her voice when she says
to Abraham,

> My *injustice*[16] be upon you. I gave my maid to your embrace.
> And see? She has conceived, while I am despised . . . . May Yahweh
> judge between me and you (Gen. 16:5).

The Sarah-Abraham-Hagar triangle breaks apart, finally, when
Abraham reluctantly permits Sarah to protect herself against
Hagar's contempt. True, he is understandably repulsed by her
cruelty toward Hagar, but he can do little to stop it. He can't simply
replace Sarah with Hagar. Nor can he stop Hagar from looking on
Sarah with contempt. Like Elkanah, the husband of Hannah and
Peninnah, Abraham is caught in something of a no-win situation.

What Abraham wants is simple. He wants an heir for his name.
He wants to leave a monument to his existence. Therefore the most
important question for him at this late stage of his life is "How
much am I willing to suffer to have a son?" "How much am I willing to tolerate from these two women?" We need to remember that
the patriarchal culture in which Abraham lives drives him to place
the production of an heir at the very center of his priority system.

ABRAHAM AS UNCLE

In Genesis 13, Abraham graciously allows Lot to keep the well-
watered land toward Sodom, while he takes for himself the less
fertile land of the northern Negeb. In chapter 14, as soon as he finds

out that his nephew has been captured by a coalition of kings, he mounts a successful expedition to rescue Lot from slavery. Refusing to take the spoils solely for himself, he insists that Mamre, Eshcol and Aner, his Amorite kinsmen, receive their fair shares as well. Up to this point Abraham appears to be an active, gracious and compassionate chieftain.

Yet when Lot's new city, Sodom, comes under imminent divine attack, Abraham does nothing at all. He mounts no rescue expedition. He takes no spoils. He doesn't even send his nephew a letter of warning. This contrasts sharply with his earlier role as Lot's protector. So by the time he does get involved, it's too late. Lot's daughters have already married Sodomites, and Lot's wife has become too fond of "life in the big city" to leave willingly.

Still, Abraham is not completely passive. He tries to do something. What we find instead of a rescue attempt, however, is a philosophical dialogue between Abraham and God over the city's fate. This is the famous passage where Abraham begins with fifty righteous persons and bargains God down to ten. God agrees not to destroy Sodom if ten righteous people can be found there. The negotiation begins with Abraham standing alone before God and ends with him going "to his place."

On the surface of things it looks like Abraham is bargaining out of compassion for his nephew. But is he? The Jewish historian Josephus claims that he is, but the text itself is conspicuously silent.[17] In fact, the only precedent we have for determining his behavior here is his previous behavior. And we have already seen that his behavior towards Sarah has as much to do with fear as it does with faith.

ABRAHAM AS FATHER

I believe this is why God makes Abraham's third test so difficult. Abraham needs to be confronted. He needs to be challenged. God's command to sacrifice Isaac forces him out of his comfort zone. It makes him decide what he really believes, whom he really trusts. It makes him reexamine his priorities like no other conflict in his life.

God's plan is clear. By this point of the narrative, he has stated and restated it to Abraham several times. God desires nothing less than to bless the world through Abraham's descendants, something Abraham cannot possibly comprehend, at least not yet. He desires to make of him a great nation, a nation of priests, a nation set apart. God wants Abraham to be the "point man" in his battle to reclaim the Creation itself from the power of the Evil One.[18]

Such a dream, however, is impossible without *faith*. God needs to know whether Abraham has it. Not simply a passive acceptance of divine power—anyone can practice *that* kind of "faith." No, what God seeks is an active devotion to the divine will. God needs to know whether Abraham has *genuine* faith. Is he committed to Yahweh and him alone, or is Yahweh just one of many deities in Abraham's Amorite pantheon?

To find out, God picks out the one thing in Abraham's life that is most precious, most tender, and most vulnerable—his desire for children—and tests *that*.

God knows how much Abraham wants a son. Yet, as with any of his blessings, he knows how utterly idolatrous the desire for children can become, left undevoted to him.[19] Thus it is interesting to watch how God leads him into parenthood.

First, he allows him to experience it through Ishmael. Then he forces him to reassess its importance with Isaac. With Ishmael, Abraham exults in the joy of first-time fatherhood. In fact, he enjoys it too much. He becomes arrogant. We see this in the scene where he mocks God. With Isaac, however, he has to learn why God gives children at all, to him or any other father.

Let's be clear. Abraham's problem is not that he loves his children. His problem is that his love for his children is misplaced. Devotion to his children threatens to blind him to the will of God.

CONFLICT RESOLUTION

The parenthood industry is booming today. Films with titles like *Parenthood, Immediate Family, Three Men and a Baby,* and *Baby Boom* have done great business at the box office and the video store. Books and articles on the subject are selling like hotcakes. The barrage is so intense I wonder sometimes whether some of us think that ours is the first generation ever to discover the joys of having children and raising families!

Infertile couples will move heaven and earth to obtain a baby, according to a recent cover story of a prominent news magazine.[20] Fertile couples can and do invest everything they have in their children, blindly ignoring what it does to them.[21] Self-help books confidently tell us how adolescents ought to parent,[22] how bachelors can transition into parenthood,[23] how parents can operate after age 30,[24] how to parent after a divorce,[25] how to survive toxic parents,[26] how to parent without a partner,[27] how to parent as a surrogate mother,[28] and even how homosexual couples can parent.[29]

Why? What is the reason for this relentless barrage? Is it to help contemporary parents learn better how to raise their children in their Father's image? Or is it because too many of us, like Abraham, are deathly afraid of leaving this earth without a memorial to ourselves and our own paltry power?

Christian parents are not immune to the sin of "parentolatry." In the name of "good parenting" I see parents punish their four-year-olds for "failing" to win at soccer, or baseball, or some other sport. In the name of good parenting, I see parents respond to a "C" on a report card like it's the beginning of World War III. In the name of good parenting, I see parents change churches solely because they want their children to experience a "better" youth group. In the name of good parenting, I see parents move heaven and earth to get their child into the "right" schools, the "right" athletic teams, the "right" social environments, yet never teach them how to pray, or study Scripture, or serve the poor.

Their priorities are too much like Abraham's. They have yet to know what it means to live by faith.

The story of Abraham has many levels and many lessons can be drawn from it. But perhaps the most relevant lesson for our age is this: Faith is not a bargain. Faith is not a negotiation. Faith is not an option. Faith is a decision to submit wholly, completely, and unreservedly to a holy God. A God who loves without conditions. A God who provides without question. A God who tests us when we go astray.

Abraham's temptation, like ours, is to worship something in place of the living God. That's why God tests *his* faith, and that's why God continues to test *ours*. Yes, the conflicts we experience as we try to parent our children in a fallen world are profound and wearisome. But if the story of Abraham teaches us anything, it is this:

Conflict resolution is impossible without faith.

QUESTIONS FOR DISCUSSION

(1) Why is it hard for Mel to reconcile with his dad?
(2) Do you know any "Sarahs"? Describe.
(3) Do you know any "Hagars"? Describe.
(4) Do you know any "Lots"? Describe.
(5) Why do we tend to immortalize people like Abraham?
(6) Why is God's test of Abraham so harsh?
(7) Why does our faith need testing?

ENDNOTES

[1]Jeffrey S. Siker discusses Abraham's image and *persona* in *Disinheriting the Jews: Abraham in Early Christian Controversy* (Louisville, KY: Westminster/John Knox, 1991).

[2]Josephus, *Antiquities of the Jews*, Book I, Chapters vii-xiii. Josephus is a Jewish historian who lived in the first century A.D. The standard English translation of his work is by William Whiston (Grand Rapids: Kregel, 1960) pp. 32-37.

[3]John A. Hutchinson, *Paths of Faith* (New York: McGraw-Hill, 1969) p. 450.

[4]Hunter Lewis discusses the strong pull of tribal morality in *A Question of Values: Six Ways We Make the Personal Choices That Shape Our Lives* (San Francisco: HarperCollins, 1990) pp. 86-97.

[5]This story is practically duplicated in Genesis 20:1-18.

[6]Warren Wiersbe emphasizes that the Latin word *integritas* means "wholeness." A person with integrity is not divided or pretending to be whole. People of integrity have nothing to hide. Their lives are open books. See *The Integrity Crisis* (Nashville: Thomas Nelson, 1988) pp. 1-12.

[7]Sarah laughs later (Genesis 18:12), but Abraham laughs first.

[8]John Gammie offers a much-needed study of God's holiness in his book *Holiness in Israel* (Minneapolis: Fortress, 1989). A review appears in *Christian Studies* 11, 1 (1990) pp. 60-70.

[9]One fact that needs to be remembered is that child sacrifice was very common among the nations surrounding Israel (2 Kings 3:27), as well as Israel itself (Jeremiah 7:31).

[10]Like Romans 4:1-25 or Hebrews 11:17-19.

[11]See his video series *Christian Marriage* (Orlando, FL: Ligonier Ministries) lesson # 6.

[12]See the classic study of Genesis 22:1-14 in Erich Auerbach's *Mimesis* (translated by Willard Trask; Princeton: Princeton University Press, 1953).

[13]Victor Kassel, "Polygyny After Sixty," in H. A. Otto, ed., *The Family in Search of a Future* (New York: Appleton-Century-Crofts, 1970) pp. 137-143.

[14]Esther, for example, probably would never have "auditioned" for Ahasuerus' harem had her economic and political circumstances not been so bleak.

[15]Marcus Jastrow refers to this rabbinic tradition in his exhaustive *Dictionary of the Targumim, the Talmud Babli and Yerushalmi, and the Midrashic Literature*, vol. 2 (Brooklyn, NY: P. Shalom, 1967) p. 1070.

[16]Literally, "violence." This word is used to describe actual murder in Judges 9:24.

[17]Josephus, *Antiquities of the Jews* I, xi, 3.

[18]For a practical application, see Steve Farrar, *Point Man: How a Man Can Lead a Family* (Portland, OR: Multnomah, 1990).

[19]On the problem of idolatrous behavior today, see C. Leonard Allen, *The Cruciform Church: Becoming a Cross-Shaped People in a Secular World*, 2nd ed. (Abilene: ACU Press, 1990) pp. 81-111.

[20]Nancy Gibbs, "The Baby Chase," Time 134, 15 (October 9, 1989) pp. 86-89. See also Miriam D. Mazor and Harriet F. Simmons, eds., *Infertility: Medical, Emotional and Social Considerations* (New York: Human Sciences Press, 1984). I hasten to add, however, that the problem of infertility needs to be handled with extreme care; see John van Regenmorter, "Let's Stop Childless Abuse," *Christianity Today* 37, 2 (Feb 8, 1993) p. 15.

[21]David Elkind, *The Hurried Child: Growing Up Too Fast, Too Soon*, 2nd ed. (Reading, MA: Addison-Wesley, 1988).

[22]Margaret K. Rosenheim and Mark F. Testa, *Early Parenthood and Coming of Age in the 1990s* (New Brunswick, NJ: Rutgers University, 1992).

[23]Phyllis W. Berman and Frank A. Pedersen, *Men's Transitions to Parenthood* (Hillsdale, NJ: L. Erlbaum Associates, 1987).

[24]Judith Blackfield Cohen, *Parenthood After 30? A Guide to Personal Choice* (Lexington, MA: Lexington Books, 1985).

[25]Ciji Ware, *Sharing Parenthood After Divorce: An Enlightened Custody Guide for Mothers, Fathers and Kids* (New York: Viking, 1982).

[26]Susan Forward and Craig Buck, *Toxic Parents: Overcoming Their Hurtful Legacy and Reclaiming Your Life* (New York: Bantam, 1989).

[27]Kathleen McCoy, *Solo Parenting: Your Essential Guide* (New York: New American Library, 1987).

[28]Herbert Richardson, ed., *On the Problem of Surrogate Parenthood: Analyzing the Baby M Case* (Lewiston, NY: Mellen Press, 1987).

[29]Friedrich W. Bozet, ed., *Gay and Lesbian Parents* (New York: Praeger, 1987).

DAVID AND HIS TEENAGERS

(2 SAMUEL 13:1-18:33)

"I just can't take it anymore."

"Take what?" I asked.

"The hypocrisy. The guilt. I feel so ashamed when I come to church. I just can't stand to see him up there week after week, leading prayers, making announcements, pretending like everything is just fine."

"You mean, even though your father's a successful businessman and a respected leader in the church, you still resent him?"

"You bet I do," he replied without hesitation. "He's a different person at home. You don't know him like I do. You just don't know."

The young man sitting across from me was going through a messy divorce. His wife had left him and had taken the children with her. He had never been self-confident enough to hold a job longer than six months in his entire life. He had stopped attending church. He was lonely.

One afternoon he called and asked to talk. Before I could even sink back in the chair he hit me with a veritable tidal wave of anger. Out of his mouth flowed a torrent of bitterness like nothing I had ever heard before. Most of his feelings were focused on his father. Not knowing much about the history of their relationship, I made a mental note to take everything he said with a grain of salt until I could confirm it later through another source.

About two months later, I had the opportunity to talk with his sister.

"Is Dad really the tyrant your brother makes him out to be?"

His sister shot me a look of utter amazement, followed immediately by a nervous, knowing laugh. "Worse," she said. "My mother used to drink herself drunk just to get away from him. I feel sorry for you. I really do. You're going to have to work with this man day after day, week after week. It's not going to be easy. I'm glad I got out from under him while I was still able."

The room suddenly felt warm, so I went over to the window and opened it. After all, this was not just any member of my congregation they were talking about. This was the man who signed my paycheck. This was one of the church's most influential leaders, a man respected by many in the congregation as well as the surrounding community. Or so I thought.

"You really have no idea what he's like, do you," she went on. Then out of her mouth came the same stories I had heard from her brother: stories of neglect, pain, heartache, and abuse. It was a long, painful afternoon. Closing our session as delicately as I could, I thanked her for her help, escorted her to the door, slunk back to my chair, and prayed out loud:

"Now what, Lord?"

This man's adult children have lost their spouses, abandoned their children, forsaken the church, and retreated into an asylum of self pity. Not too long after these interviews I learned of the mother's death, the victim of an alcohol-related disease which, according to the children, had resulted from their father's abuse. His brand of "leadership" had done irreparable damage to his family.

Jesus says we can tell the wolves from the shepherds by the fruits they bear (Matt. 7:16). Well, the fruits of this man are painfully abundant. Besides the damage to his family, he has left in his wake a church whose sense of mission has died, whose benevolent outreach has shriveled up, whose joy in worship has vanished, and whose vision of the Kingdom is twisted and petty.

Here's an exercise you might try sometime when you've got nothing to do. Call an older minister and ask him what his first one or two churches were like. Perhaps he will tell you that he had the good fortune to start his ministry in a relatively mature church under godly leaders. Then again, maybe you'll hear a different story. Maybe you'll hear a story like the one you've just read.

The Dean of Seaver College at Pepperdine University put the issue bluntly in a recent speech. Churches of Christ everywhere are facing nothing less than a "crisis of leadership" that's getting worse by the day.[1] What lies at the root of this crisis? How do men like the one just described get to be religious leaders in local churches? Why do churches willingly hand over the reins of responsibility to them? Certainly there are many leaders today who work hard at maintaining a credible congruence between spiritual parenting and spiritual leadership.[2] But too often it is the self-willed who take the reins, not the surrendered. Further, this problem is nurtured and compounded by the fact that we live in an age where apathy is rampant, accountability remains largely undefined, and mediocrity is the only thing left to fill up the vacuum.[3]

Countless fellowships of God's people are suffering today as a result of this leadership crisis.

THE STORY

Scripture is filled with stories about strong men and women who fail as parents, and David's relationship to his teenagers is one of the most memorable. With Absalom, David gives his son a name which means "father of peace," but the name *ab-shalom* is prophetically ironic. This father and this son experience little real peace over the course of their relationship. Instead, there is passivity, manipulation, paralysis, anger, bitterness, and unrelenting conflict. Their story is not a pretty one. The manner in which it ends is almost unbelievably tragic. Yet it needs to be examined today because in it God speaks directly and comprehensively to the spiritual leadership crisis which now afflicts his people.[4]

The story begins with a terrible act of violence. Amnon rapes his half-sister Tamar, and this crime sets the tone for a series of unspeakable horrors. When Absalom, Tamar's full brother, finds out about the rape, he turns to David for justice. David, however, is in a delicate political position because Amnon is the crown prince of the kingdom. More than that, he is the son of Ahinoam, a northern, Ephraimite woman. Absalom and Tamar are children of Maacah, a non-Israelite. Amnon's welfare, because he is more ethnically "pure," is therefore more important to David than Tamar's.[5]

Astonishingly, David does nothing to punish Amnon for his criminal behavior. Thus, David's passivity drives Absalom to take matters into his own hands. He plots revenge against Amnon. Two full years later, he ambushes his brother, has him killed at a public ceremony, and flees the country.

Again, David does nothing. Three more years pass, and he gingerly invites his son back from exile, under pressure from Joab, his general. Yet when Absalom accepts the invitation and returns to Jerusalem, David refuses to allow him back into the precincts of the royal court (again, probably for political reasons). This leads to further retaliation from Absalom, and finally to a civil war between a rebel-party led by Absalom and a loyalist-party led by David.

All told, there are at least three significant moments when David and Absalom try to communicate in this fascinating, tragic story, either personally or through an intermediary. Each meeting between them becomes increasingly difficult as their relationship stumbles, trips, and falls into a dark abyss.

PROTECTING TAMAR

The first meeting occurs when Absalom takes Tamar out of the king's house and into his own. For all the good this may do for Tamar, it does precious little good for Absalom's relationship to David. In fact, this act of Absalom's is a public slap in David's face. In Israel, or any other patriarchal culture, a woman does not ordinarily leave her father's house until marriage. The function of *protector* is an important one. Boaz, for example, goes to a great deal of trouble to protect Ruth (Ruth 2:8-16). Jacob's sons try to protect their sister Dinah, albeit unsuccessfully, from Canaanite defilement (Gen. 34:14).

Thus, by taking Tamar out prematurely, Absalom short-circuits this process and embarrasses his father. By taking Tamar out of her father's house, though his intentions may have been honorable, Absalom profoundly challenges David's role as Tamar's protector.

SUSPICION

Two years later, Absalom holds a sheep shearing party, and invites his father to attend. Twice, in fact, he "presses" him to attend.[6] The word for "press" is an interesting choice here, a term when seen in context is pregnant with suspense. Most often it is found in parallel passages where horrifying events are predicted. Lot, for example, "presses" the two angels who visit him to leave Sodom's streets before nightfall (Gen. 19:3). The father-in-law of the travelling Levite at the end of Judges "presses" his son-in-law not to go out at night into the wild streets of Gibeah (Judg. 19:7).[7]

In an eerily similar way, Absalom "presses" his father to come to Ephraim, perhaps in the hope that the king will do something to address Absalom's legitimate grievance toward Amnon. Should David relent and go to the ceremony, much bloodshed could probably be avoided.

Again, however, David passively refuses to get involved with his kids. Absalom "presses" him, then, to send Amnon in his place. To this request, David asks Absalom a question which brings their whole relationship into sudden, disturbing focus.

"Why should Amnon go with you?"

This looks like an innocent enough request, but look at it carefully. With this question, the narrator forces us to see a side of David that perhaps we would rather not see. We as readers know why Absalom wants Amnon to attend this ceremony. The narrator knows why. Absalom knows why. Probably every member of David's court knows why. Yet David *still* doesn't know why. He doesn't seem to know what's going on at all. He is *that* detached from the affairs of his teenagers.

With this question, Absalom's plan begins to leak into our minds like some deadly poisonous gas. By bringing it to such overt attention, the narrator wants to make us feel the pressure building in the relationship between this father and this son. An uneasy suspicion is ever-so-subtly beginning to divide them from one another, a suspicion which mushrooms into distrust, then rebellion, then bloody civil war.

TOTAL ABDICATION

Years pass, and the king yearns for Absalom's return. Why? Because with Amnon dead, Absalom's political status has dramatically changed. Absalom is the new crown prince, the new "son of David," the next heir apparent to the throne of Israel. David knows that the intensity of the conflict between himself and his son has now become secondary to a larger, more pressing question: Who will be the next king of Israel?

Communication breakdown between a father and son is one thing. National paralysis is quite another.

At least this is how Joab thinks, one of the most ruthless characters in all of Scripture. Ever the pragmatist, Joab cares nothing about David's domestic crisis. He cares only about the precarious state of the nation, now floundering under a passive monarch. For Joab, David's problem is political survival, pure and simple. His only choice is to decide between the lesser of two evils. Either do nothing and watch the kingdom deteriorate into anarchy, or bring Absalom back to Jerusalem and take your chances on some kind of dynastic succession.

Both Israel and her enemies are intensely interested in seeing what the king will decide to do.

Notice that Joab does not even *attempt* to appeal to David's paternal nature. Perhaps he thinks, after watching David's cold reaction to the rape of his daughter and the murder of his son, that such an approach would be a waste of time anyway. Nowhere does he suggest that the king and the prince simply talk it out "father to son." Nowhere does he suggest that the king pray or inquire of the Lord. Instead he tries a shrewdly calculating scheme to refocus David's attention on the "real" issue. He hires a "wise woman" to help David make a decision about a hypothetical situation in the hope that David will also make a political decision to bring Absalom home.

Well, it works. Absalom does come back to Jerusalem, even though David still refuses to allow him into his presence. The question we want to ask of David at this point in the story is "Why?" Why does David act like this? Why is he so passively cautious, almost to the point of political paralysis? Why does he seem to be so convinced, up to this point, that his conflict with Absalom can be resolved by purely political means, yet later, when Absalom is killed, we see his other, compassionate side come to full fruition?[8]

In other words, why does David, like most ambivalent fathers, think that the the easiest way out of his dilemma is simply to deny that there is one?

CONFLICT RESOLUTION

Bill Cosby knows how fathers feel:

"Parents are not really interested in justice. They just want quiet."[9]

And we do. Sometimes all we want is to sit down and read the newspaper. We're tired. We've worked hard all day. The last thing we want to hear about is Alice poking her finger in Rachel's eye or Johnny cutting off part of his brother's ear while giving him a haircut. We're not in the mood to hear about how Susie got bitten by the neighbor's Doberman, or how Jimmy ran his bike into the rear of a parked car and broke his nose in two places.

> We have always been against calling the children idiots. This philosophy has been basic for my wife and me. And we proudly lived by it until the children came along.[10]

Sometimes, however, the weariness fathers often feel can degenerate into something more sinister: passivity and denial. When this happens, we have a problem on our hands—because passivity, like David's, can lead to full-fledged detachment.

Then things are not so funny. When children are neglected, ignored or abused by this passivity, communication can break down and love can dry up. We can then choose to bury our heads in sand which is a little too deep. We spend more time on our work than we should. We find excuses for putting off that family vacation. We avoid supporting our children's activities, or even talking to them about their homework. All parents, if we're honest with ourselves, can readily understand the causes behind David's weariness, ambivalence and indecisiveness.

But rape? Murder? Incest?

Where do we draw the line between involvement and detachment? Does David know when he's crossed it? Do we?

But let's get down to the nitty-gritty. How do we, as ministers of reconciliation, apply a story like this to a world of single parent families and deadbeat fathers? How can this story make sense to a world which is teeming with adolescent gangs—those desperate, twisted family-substitutes which grow like a fungus on dead family relationships, only poorly replacing the nurture, authority, and love

of real parents?[11]

Some of the kids in my church have never even seen their biological fathers. Countless others have never had a grandfather, an uncle, or a father figure in their lives for a single day. This means that the children in these families do not know how to detach themselves fully from their infantile dependence on others. They do not know how to control their growing anger and aggression. They do not know how to work within prescribed boundaries. Research psychologists are increasingly discovering that none of these traits have a chance of forming in the lives of these troubled kids because none of these kids has ever had a *father* actively involved in their lives.[12]

Others do have fathers at home, but instead of love, some of the children in our churches live in constant fear of being attacked by men whose idea of "discipline" is little more than child abuse.[13]

Take the Jahnke family, for example. Richard Jahnke, an agent for the Internal Revenue Service, abused his family so brutally that his sixteen-year-old son Richie felt he had to murder him in order to protect himself and his sister from abuse. One cold winter's night in Cheyenne, Wyoming, Richie took his dad's 12-gauge shotgun, met him at the garage door, and pulled the trigger.

At the trial, Richie testified that his father regularly scrubbed his sister's acne-scarred face until it bled, that he habitually beat his mother to a bloody pulp, that he sometimes played a "game" at home where he walked around the house with a handgun strapped to his side, daring anyone to make a move. All in the name of "discipline." The jury was so moved by his testimony that in spite of the violent nature of his crime, Richie was given only two years in prison, a sentence which sparked a storm of controversy on both sides of the child abuse question.[14]

The Jahnke case may be extreme, but the abuse it characterizes is distressingly common. This case raises, along with thousands of others just like it,[15] a number of disturbing questions. Perhaps the most pressing one for our age is this: "How can a father allow his relationship to his children to drift into chaos?" More to the point, "How can the fathers among us avoid the same tragedy?"

Busy fathers like you and me need constantly to be on our guards lest we lose perspective. Freelance journalist Lawrence

Wright keeps a cartoon tacked to his wall which helps him, and I commend it to you. It's a picture of a man stuffed in a cannon. His face is directed toward the clouds, and one of his hands is popping out to light the fuse. The caption underneath reads simply:

AMBITION.[16]

Wright has his finger on the pulse, doesn't he? Let's be honest. Some of us have an almost addictive compulsion to lapse into workaholism, even when our families and churches need our leadership, because all of our attention is centered on our careers, not our families. All of our attention is centered on our jobs, not our vocations. The reason why Wright has this cartoon tacked to his wall is because he knows where his weakness is. He knows he needs to look at this cartoon every day because he knows he needs a daily reminder that his job is not the most important thing in his life.

Fyodor Dostoyevsky began his journalistic career by condemning the authoritarianism of the Russian monarchy, particularly the repulsive behavior of Czar Alexander I. He ended his career by turning back (like Plato and other philosophers) to his conservative roots, eventually even writing a political rationale for the monarchy. In his later years, Dostoyevsky even tried to convince himself that "the filial love of the people for the czar" would be enough to protect Russia from the Communists. Surely, he reasoned in an op-ed piece for a Russian newspaper, "the children will not betray their father."[17]

Apparently the same blind belief in paternal authority seems to lie at the root of David's parenting philosophy. For all the good he does for Israel, David never seems to learn that paternal authority is something one *earns*, not something one *commands*. Thus the lesson of this story is clear. If we want our children to respect our authority, then we're going to have to *earn* it from them, not coerce it. We're going to have to win their love and respect in a way that does not alienate, confuse, or humiliate them in the process.[18]

Additionally, this story shows us how badly we need to point our children upward and inspire them if we expect them to succeed. We need to think out and implement a clear-cut spiritual plan for their lives and our own. We have to set realistic, challenging goals. We have to be willing to evaluate ourselves honestly to see whether we're still on track with these goals. We have to be willing to take constructive criticism for the sake of our children's spiritual salvation.[19]

In sum, when David utterly fails his children in all three of these areas—*communication, discipline* and *spiritual planning*—the results are chaos and division. Israel's most bloody, heinous, and needless civil war grows out of a single unresolved conflict between a father and his son. This story stands as a sharp reminder to every Christian parent of just how high the price can be when we choose to leave our conflicts unresolved.

No father can afford to wait until his children are spiritually, emotionally, or physically dead before he opens up his heart to them and tells them he loves them.

> *O my son Absalom!*
> *My son!*
> *My son Absalom!*
> *Would I had died instead of you!*
> *O Absalom!*
> *My son!*
> *My son!*

QUESTIONS FOR DISCUSSION

(1) Why do you think David detached from his children?

(2) What could he have done about it? When? Why?

(3) Without naming names, do you know any "Absaloms"? Describe.

(4) Do you know any "Tamars"? Describe.

(5) How do you feel about Joab's attempt at conflict resolution?

(6) How would you have counseled Absalom?

(7) Why do you think this story was preserved in the Bible?

ENDNOTES

[1]John F. Wilson, "Saints, Shepherds, Preachers, and Scholars: Leadership Crisis in Churches of Christ," *Restoration Quarterly* 34 (1992) pp. 129-134.

[2]A connection repeatedly emphasized in the Pastoral letters of the New Testament (see 1 Timothy 3:1-7; Titus 1:5-9).

[3]Isaiah 3:4 speaks of a time when leadership was similarly poor: "I will make boys their princes, and babes shall rule over them." For a contemporary critique, see Max De Pree's penetrating diagnosis in *Leadership is An Art* (New York: Doubleday, 1989) pp. 9-19.

[4]For further study from the book of Jeremiah, see M. S. Moore, "Jeremiah's Identity Crisis," *Restoration Quarterly* 34 (1992) pp. 135-149.

[5]On the power of ethnicity to shape values, see Hunter Lewis, *A Question of Values* (San Francisco: Harper, 1990) pp. 86-97.

[6]Here I am reading 2 Samuel 14:25 with a fragment of the Samuel text discovered in the famous Dead Sea Scrolls.

[7]On this story, see the sensitive reading by Phyllis Trible, *Texts of Terror* (Philadelphia: Fortress, 1984) pp. 65-92.

[8]Hearing the news of Absalom's death, David laments his son in a way that astonishes us with its intensity (2 Samuel 18:33).

[9]Bill Cosby, *Fatherhood* (Garden City, NY: Doubleday, 1986) p. 54.
[10]*Ibid.*

[11]Gordon Witkin, "Kids Who Kill," *U. S. News and World Report* 110 (April 8, 1991) pp. 26-32. Carl S. Taylor publishes actual interviews with gang members in *Dangerous Society* (East Lansing, MI: Michigan State University, 1990) pp. 48-57.

[12]The characteristics just described are a direct result of father-deprivation, according to research cited by John W. Miller, *Biblical Faith and Fathering: Why We Call God "Father"* (New York: Paulist Press, 1989) pp. 13-39. One of Miller's main contentions is that the father-involved family has always been a precarious cultural achievement, an achievement constantly threatened by the biological tendency in all human cultures to exclude fathers in favor of mothers only. For further study, see George Guilder, *Men and Marriage* (Gretna, LA: Pelican, 1993).

[13]Gilda Berger estimates that at least 300,000 and perhaps as many as 600,000 children are victims of physical abuse each year in the United States; *Violence and the Family* (New York: Franklin Watts, 1990) p. 54.

[14]Cited in Greggory W. Morris, *The Kids Next Door: Sons and Daughters Who Kill Their Parents* (New York: William Morrow and Co., 1985) pp. 117-119.

[15]On Feb 5, 1993 two sisters, ages 12 and 11, shot their adoptive mother to death in a housing project close to Phoenix, Arizona. Sources close to the family said that when the adoptive mother was approached by officials of the state Child Protective Services about her abusive behavior, she told them she could "hit her children if she wanted," and "if they didn't like it, they knew where the door was." *The Arizona Republic* (March 20, 1993) pp. A1, A11.

[16]Lawrence Wright, "I Want To Be Alone," *Texas Monthly* 13 (December, 1985) p. 166.

[17]Cited in W. A. Visser't Hooft, *The Fatherhood of God In An Age of Emancipation* (Philadelphia: Westminster, 1982) p. 22.

[18]M. Scott Peck, *A World Waiting to be Born* (New York: Bantam, 1993) pp. 147-172.

[19]*Ibid.*

MIRIAM'S ERROR

(EXODUS 2:1-10; NUMBERS 12:1-15)

"I want to get along with her, but she makes me feel so . . . *inadequate*. She always finds something wrong with me. If I don't vacuum the house every day, it's not clean enough. If one of the kids has a cold, then I don't take good enough care of her grandchildren. If Bob looks even the *least* bit unhappy, then I'm not a good enough wife. It doesn't matter what I do! I'm *never* good enough for this woman! *Never!*"

Janet's conflict is not in her mind. It's very real. Like a festering boil, it badly needs to be lanced and drained. Springs of healing need to be identified. Avenues of hope need reopening. While she weeps, my wife and I wearily, instinctively drop our heads:

"Lord, please help Janet. Please help her endure this cross. Please give her the strength to do what's right."

Mary, Janet's mother-in-law, is at it again. Grinding down yet another soul in her relentless drive for legal perfection. The god she idealizes looks very little like the biblical God. The pattern she follows with Janet and others usually goes something like this: Mary sees something she feels is "wrong." Immediately she confronts the perpetrator of this "wrong." Invariably she offends this person, who either cries out for help, works out the conflict privately, or leaves the church.

Janet has no idea how to deal with her. None of us do, really. Most Christians who have been burned by her acid tongue simply avoid her. Mary has few real friends. Even her family finds her difficult. As the newest member of that family, Janet knows it's going to be tough. She knows how dangerous it can be to cross her. What she doesn't know is whether she has the grit to endure. She wonders how much she can take of Mary.

Janet's "mistake" was this. Of all the people she could have chosen to marry, she chose Mary's son. By marrying Bob, Janet became part of Mary's family, living on her turf, subject to her rules. With the words "I do," every relationship, every plan, every dream, every activity, every facet of her life became subject overnight to Mary's intense, microscopic scrutiny.

It's crippling her emotionally and spiritually. Trying to keep her sense of humor, she's hoping things will eventually get better. Yet the pressure is great, the prejudice against her deeply ingrained. Mary's will is stronger than hers, and they both know it.

From Mary's point of view, Janet is not at all the "proper" daughter-in-law she had long imagined for her oldest son. In fact, she is bitterly disappointed with Bob for marrying her at all, and tells him so as often as she can. Her self-appointed mission now is to make the most of a "bad" situation. She sees herself as Janet's drill sergeant. She sees it as her job to discipline Janet into the wife he *should* have chosen.

Life in Mary's shadow was so oppressive and so shame-filled when Janet came to us, that she was actually beginning to have fantasies about taking her own life. She once said,

"You know how much Mary likes quilts, right? Well, sometimes *I* feel like a quilt. To Mary, I'll never be a beautiful tapestry. I'm just a ragged old blanket stashed away in the attic somewhere. My colors are fading, my fabric is threadbare, and my edges are fraying badly. So to her I need to be kept away from public view."

Winston Churchill once called the Soviet Union a "question wrapped in a riddle clothed in an enigma." Well, Sister Mary is *our* "Soviet Union," our enigma. She says she "loves the Lord." Yet no one really knows what "loving the Lord" means to her. In her own strange, idiosyncratic way, she tries to help others. To her credit, she visits more hospitals and sends more cards to the bereaved than anyone else in the congregation. She cleans the baptistry regularly. She organizes showers for expectant mothers. She performs many good works in the name of Jesus.

But she never lets you forget it, either. For example, Mary will make a hospital visit in the morning, then gossip in the afternoon that the minister or elders don't care about so-and-so because no one has made a visit yet, except her. I've seen her publicly rebuke a youth minister before a crowd of visitors, then wonder why he decides to leave the ministry. To a group of college students dreaming of doing mission work in Europe, she asks, "When are you going to get *serious* about your lives and find *real* jobs like everyone else?" On the night of Janet's baptism she was overheard whispering to onlookers, "She's only doing this to draw attention to herself."

Other examples might be cited, but there's no need to belabor the point. Mary is the kind of person who goes to church every Sunday, who gives of her means, who attends all the Bible classes, who visits the sick, who brings food to the "pot-lucks" . . . *and still believes that she deserves to be saved.* Around her, people are constantly forced to "walk on eggs." You'll never hear Mary say the healing words "I'm sorry." You'll never hear her say the most precious words in the Christian faith: "I forgive you."

In short, Mary personifies one of the most subtle, devastating conflicts now afflicting Christ's church: devotion without penitence, piety without forgiveness, law without grace.[1]

Our heart goes out to Janet. She has indeed married into a legalistic matriarchy, distorted in form and misguided in purpose.[2] And we don't have the heart to agree with her that Mary might change. Too many broken and bleeding souls lie strewn in her wake for us to think otherwise.

Yet she can still do something about her situation. She can still pray for endurance. She can still open up her heart to a Suffering God and receive a measure of spiritual strength.[3] She can still pray that her mother-in-law might somehow grow in her understanding of grace (Rom. 5:18-21).

She can also spend time reflecting on Scripture, especially those stories in the Bible where individuals much like herself undergo similar challenges of intolerance and oppression.

Moses' conflict with Miriam is one of those stories.

THE STORY

Miriam receives little attention in early Christian circles. Nothing significant is said about her in the New Testament.[4] Nor is much said about her in early Christian literature outside the New

Testament.[5] This silence is rather strange, not least because it stands in such stark contrast to the lavish attention she receives from another, unexpected source. The *rabbis*—an entrenched bastion of male chauvinism if ever there was one—regard her highly. Indeed, the rabbis revere Miriam as a "mother in Israel."

Much of the attention she receives from this source centers on a single reference from the book of Micah:

> Oh my people, what have I done to you? In what have I wearied you? Answer me! I brought you up from the land of Egypt. I redeemed you from the house of bondage. I sent Moses, Aaron and Miriam before you (Micah 6:3-4).

Many a rabbi has agonized over this passage. Their problem in a nutshell seems to be this: How can Micah give Miriam equal billing? How can he list her alongside Moses and Aaron, two of Israel's greatest heroes? What about Joshua? What about Samuel? Why aren't they mentioned? Are they somehow less important? Is there some "secret" reason for her inclusion here?

Miriam is a profound puzzle to the rabbis. And if you know anything about ancient Judaism, then you know how much they love a good puzzle. Explanations for her inclusion in Micah are many and varied.[6] For example, Yose ben Yehuda, in his comments on Numbers 20:1-2, tries to explain it like this:

> Three good pillars stood in Israel: Moses, Aaron, and Miriam. Three good gifts were given through them. They are the fountain, the pillar of cloud, and the manna. The fountain, on account of Miriam's service, the pillar of cloud, on account of Aaron's service. The manna, on account of Moses' service. When Miriam died, the fountain disappeared, as it was said, "There Miriam died." After that, it is said, "And there was no water for the congregation there."

This is a quotation from the *Babylonian Talmud*, a document about as sacred to Jews as the writings of church fathers like Irenaeus and Clement are to Roman Catholics.[7] Because it contains an "official" explanation of Miriam's prominence, it needs to be considered carefully and weighed judiciously. Not only does it draw a direct connection between Miriam's death and Israel's loss of water in the wilderness, it goes on to argue that her "gift" is at least as important as the "gifts" of her more famous siblings.

The Talmud is strange. From our point of view, ben Yehuda seems to be reading Numbers 20:1-2 in a forced way. We westerners don't read Scripture like this. We don't make what we would probably consider "unwarranted" connections, that is, connections not defensible from the historical and literary context of Numbers. The death of Miriam and the "death" of a water source have no inherent *historical* connection at all from our point of view. Thus we need to study carefully how the rabbis read Scripture in the first century if we want to appreciate better what ben Yehuda is trying to do with this text.[8]

Yet his overall point seems as impossible to miss as it is faithful to Micah. Sister Miriam is a very important character in Israelite history. Just look at her. She helps to preserve Moses' life at the beginning of Exodus (Exod. 2:1-10). Crossing the Sea to escape Pharaoh, she leads Israel in praise and worship as a Hebrew "prophetess" (Exod. 15:20-21) Centuries later she is still highly regarded, revered in the same breath, in fact, as Moses and Aaron (Micah 6:4).

No wonder the rabbis puzzle over her. Her majesty grows with every Scriptural reference. Following this trajectory, a few rabbis see no harm in taking the the next logical step and embellishing her legend even further. Transcending the bounds of history, they invent a tradition about Miriam's "fountain," a tradition which grows and grows until she becomes something like the "Wonder Woman" of Talmudic history. Some rabbis practically worship her as a goddess, very much the way that some Catholics worship Mary and some Protestants worship Sophia.[9]

The portrayal in Numbers 12, however, is not at all like the rose-colored picture we see in the rabbis. Nor is it like the majestic portrayals in Exodus and Micah. Instead, what we see in Numbers is a jealous, willful woman who attempts to take advantage of a ticklish situation in order to seize power from God's "servant."[10] In response, we see an angry God strike her with leprosy, then ostracize her from the Israelite community for seven full days.

In other words, we see a side of Miriam in Numbers that is considerably less complimentary than those found elsewhere.

Why?

MOSES' BIG SISTER

Harry S. Truman faced the fight of his political life in 1952. He wanted Averill Harriman, a patrician diplomat from New York, to succeed him as President of the United States. Like politicians everywhere, his strategy was to attack the record of his opponent. Pugnacious and defiant, Truman stood up on national television and warned the Democratic convention that Adlai Stevenson, while urbane and polished, didn't stand a chance of beating General Dwight D. Eisenhower in the general election.

Stung by the charge, Stevenson called in one of his staunchest supporters to defend his honor. Her name was Eleanor. More than just a former First Lady, Mrs. Roosevelt had earned a solid reputation as a politician in her own right, particularly at the United Nations where she had worked hard on behalf of universal human rights. Immediately she postponed her vacation, flew to Chicago, and held an historic press conference.

Speaking to "more reporters and more cameramen than I had ever seen before," she answered Truman point-for-point. Cool and composed, she reminded her audience that Stevenson had been the candidate to fight for Civil Rights legislation, not Harriman. Further, Stevenson was "much better equipped" to handle foreign affairs than Harriman. Slapping Truman in his public face, she then added, "or his patron."

Harriman was stunned. Truman was speechless. This speech was the turning point for Stevenson's campaign. True, he eventually lost the general election to Eisenhower anyway, but this takes nothing away from Eleanor Roosevelt's accomplishment. A widowed First Lady had taken on the President of the United States, and beat him at his own game!

Her strength, however, was also her weakness.

Eight years and two Presidential defeats later, she tried again to persuade Stevenson to make a run for the White House. Against the advice of her sons and advisors, she went to Los Angeles to draft Stevenson onto a ballot he neither solicited nor desired—and was soundly thrashed by a well-heeled, well-oiled machine named "Kennedy." Blinded by her convictions, she failed to see what everyone else saw. In spite of his Roman Catholicism, John

Kennedy was immensely popular with the party and the public.[11] Richard Nixon would, according to the polls, crush Stevenson in the general election. Besides, Adlai Stevenson represented the goals and ideals of the "old" party, her husband's party.

Her convictions got the best of her. Kennedy won the nomination on the first ballot, and Mrs. Roosevelt sulked for weeks afterward, angry that her candidate had lost.[12]

Both women, Miriam and Eleanor, are women of uncommon intelligence. Both operate at the highest levels in national affairs. Both are well-loved by the public. Both have the courage to take a stand on the basis of principle. And both can be blinded by the untempered clarity of their own convictions.

In fact, the first time we see Miriam, she is *literally* "taking a stand"—in hip-deep mud to protect her baby brother (Exod. 2:4). Choosing her moment, she conveniently "suggests" a nurse for the child, then goes and gets the child's mother to do the job. God used Moses' sister in a powerful way. Had she not had the courage to go into dangerous waters, had she not been obedient to her mother's wishes, had she not had the intelligence to manage this situation to her family's benefit, the Exodus from Egypt might conceivably never have occurred.

I believe the word used to describe this "stand" is an important one. Most often we find it in what might be called "conviction-under-pressure" scenes in the book of Exodus. Moses "takes a stand" against Pharaoh, demanding Israel's release from slavery (Exod. 8:16). Later he commands Israel to "take a stand" at the waters of the sea and trust God to release them from Pharaoh's grasp (Exod. 14:3). Trembling and afraid, Israel "takes a stand" at the foot of Mt. Sinai as the mountain quakes and the voice of God speaks, terrifying them into awful silence (Exod. 19:17).

Miriam's "stand," in other words, is the first of many "stands" in Exodus, no less important than any other.

MOSES' ACCUSER

Yet even as Miriam's "stand" inaugurates a series of stands in Exodus, her attack against Moses launches a series of attacks in Numbers. Immediately following Numbers 12, in fact, three more challenges spring up, each more sinister than its predecessor. Ten spies try to force Moses to go back to Egypt (Num. 14:1-10). Korah, Dathan and Abiram challenge him to surrender his authority altogether at Kadesh (Num. 16:1-35). Thousands "play the harlot" and "eat sacrifices to the dead" on the plains of Moab in a passage which ranks as the "Dead Sea" of Israelite history (Num. 25:1-18).[13]

In other words, Miriam's defiance seems to start a ball rolling which almost destroys Israel. It is *because* of her great influence, not in spite of it, that other, lesser Israelites become bold enough to rebel against Moses' authority. The very manner in which this story is structured makes us ask whether Korah, or Dathan, or the ten spies, or the Moab idolaters would have challenged Moses' authority at all, had Miriam not opened the door.

In other words, this is not a story about power *denied*. It's a story about power *abused*. Miriam's problem is not that she has no authority at all. She's already a "prophetess" in Israel. She already has a significant amount of power. Her problem, like our own, is that she confuses her view of power with God's view of power. Thus she makes the critical mistake of judging others, like her brother Moses, by an inadequate yardstick: herself. She fails to understand the impact of her example. She fails to see that even prophecy has its limits.[14] She fails to recognize that Moses is much more than a prophet in the eyes of Yahweh.

> If there is a prophet among you, I Yahweh make myself known to him in a vision. I speak with him in a dream. Not so with my servant Moses. He is entrusted with all my house. With him I speak mouth to mouth, clearly, not in obscure terms. Why then were you not afraid to speak against my servant Moses? (Num. 12:6-8).

Therefore, just as Jesus has to discipline Peter in Matthew 16:23 and John 21:15-22, so Yahweh has to discipline Miriam here in Numbers 12:9-15. He strikes her with leprosy and social disgrace not because he enjoys it, and certainly not because her desire to exercise her own God-given gifts is illegitimate. He disciplines her because she fails to respect the unique character of Moses' leadership as well as her own powerful influence over others with respect to it.[15]

CONFLICT RESOLUTION

Russell Baker had a demanding mother. Growing up in the Depression, he writes poignantly of what life was like in her house. Mom was a lively woman, prone to proverbs and aphorisms at the slightest provocation. One of her favorites was, "Russell, you've got no more gumption than a bump on a log! Don't you want to amount to something?"[16]

Of course, much of what she gave to Russell did stimulate him to work hard. She did help him to develop a desire to "make something of himself."

But even when he did succeed, her reaction was the same.

> In 1954 I was assigned to cover the White House. For most reporters, being White House correspondent was as close to heaven as you could get. I was then twenty-nine years old and getting the White House job so young puffed me up with pride. I went over to Baltimore to see my mother's delight while telling her about it. I should have known better. "Well, Russ," she said, "if you work hard at this White House job you might be able to make something of yourself."[17]

The Good Times is an amusing book, chocked full of anecdotes and stories, Baker's trademark. Yet it has a darker side, too. One passage in particular sounds exactly like something Janet would say about Mary.

> On bad mornings, in the darkness, suspended between dreams and daybreak, with my mother racketing around in my head, I feel crushed by failure. I am a fool to think I amount to anything.[18]

Here's the point I'm trying to make. The church is full of women like Miriam, "Mary," and Russell's mother. Janet is not the first to suffer a godly woman's well-meaning, yet rigidly legalistic maternalism. Moses suffered from it, and perhaps you have too. Miriam never learned how to "let him go." Similarly, Mary never learned how to let Janet go and be herself—not just her daughter-in-law—*herself.*

Big sisters always mean well. Moms who *smother* instead of *mother* mean well, too. They don't intend to hurt anybody. They simply do not understand the meaning of grace. "Meaning well" is not enough. "Meaning well" is no excuse for inflicting pain. "Meaning well" is not forgiveness. "Meaning well" is not grace. Sister Miriam needs to learn this. She needs to learn how to submit her powerful will to the will of God and the church. She needs to learn how to surrender control. Most importantly, she needs to learn how to say, "I'm sorry." She needs to learn how to say, "I forgive you." Until she comes to the point in her life where she can honestly trust in a God of grace as well as a God of order, a God of mercy as well as a God of justice, her conflict with the "Janets" of this world will remain unresolved.

And she *still* won't know what to do about her daughter-in-law.

QUESTIONS FOR DISCUSSION

(1) What is Mary's problem?
(2) What is Janet's problem?
(3) What is Miriam's problem?
(4) What is Yose ben Yehuda's problem?
(5) Why do the rabbis turn Miriam into a goddess-figure?
(6) Why doesn't Russell Baker's mother praise him?
(7) Why does God punish Miriam so harshly?

ENDNOTES

[1]K. C. Haugk and R. Scott Perry elaborate this point further in *Antagonists in the Church* (Minneapolis: Augsburg, 1988). I am indebted to Terry Burgess for this reference.

[2]See further George Guilder, *Men and Marriage* (Gretna, LA: Pelican, 1993) pp. 29-38; and John W. Miller, *Biblical Faith and Fathering: Why We Call God "Father"* (New York: Paulist, 1989) pp. 13-19.

[3]See Terence E. Fretheim, *The Suffering of God: An Old Testament Perspective* (Philadelphia: Fortress, 1984).

[4]In fact, her name does not even appear in the New Testament.

[5]Her name does not even appear in the index to Edgar Hennecke and William Schneemelcher, *New Testament Apocrypha*, vol. 2 (Philadelphia: Westminster, 1965) p. 839.

[6]Adin Steinsaltz offers a pithy introduction to the world of rabbinic literature in *The Essential Talmud* (New York: Bantam, 1976). *Restoration Quarterly* has a review in volume 25 (1982) pp. 110-111.

[7]The standard English edition of the Babylonian Talmud is published in New York by the Soncino Press. Yose ben Yehuda's comment is found in the section of Talmud called *Taanith*, paragraph 9, column a.

[8]Richard Longenecker discusses this further in *Biblical Exegesis in the Apostolic Period* (Grand Rapids: Eerdmans, 1975) pp. 19-50.

[9]The Babyonian Talmud records a couple of these discussions in the sections called *Buba Metzia*, paragraph 86, column b and *Shabbat*, paragraph 35, column a. Marina Warner discusses Mary's rise to goddess-like status in *Alone of All Her Sex: The Myth and the Cult of the Virgin Mary* (New York: Random House, 1976). Elizabeth Achtemeier discusses the rise of Sophia religion in mainline Protestantism in "Why God is Not Mother," *Christianity Today* 37, 9 (Aug 16, 1993) pp. 16-20. For further study, see my reviews of *Goddesses in Religions and Modern Debate* by Larry Hurtado, ed., and *In the Wake of the Goddesses* by Tikva Frymer-Kensky in *Interpretation* 47 (1993) pp. 178-181.

[10]Karl Rengstorf points out that the term "servant" can be an honorary title for "those men in the history of Israel who have satisfied the divine claim on them in an outstanding and exemplary manner" in the *Theological Dictionary of the New Testament*, vol. 2 (Grand Rapids: Eerdmans, 1964) p. 268.

[11]Kennedy had just published his enormously popular book, *Profiles in*

Courage, which some historians feel was ghost-written by Theodore Sorenson.

[12]Joseph P. Lash, *Eleanor: The Years Alone* (New York: Norton, 1972) pp. 254-301.

[13]The Dead Sea is the lowest point on the face of the earth.

[14]Read 1 Kings 13:1-25 for a pointed story about these limits.

[15]Mary Hayter discusses the intentions and boundaries of Miriam's power in *The New Eve in Christ: The Use and Abuse of the Bible in the Debate about Women in the Church* (Grand Rapids: Eerdmans, 1987) pp. 62-63. Carroll D. Osburn discusses the problem of defining "authority" from a biblical perspective in *Women in the Church: Refocusing the Discussion* (Abilene: Restoration Perspectives, 1994) pp. 15-36, 117-122.

[16]Russell Baker, *The Good Times* (New York: Morrow, 1989) p. 7.

[17]*Ibid.,* pp. 7-8.

[18]*Ibid.,* p. 7.

JACOB'S RIVALRY

(GENESIS 25:19-33:17)

The telephone rings with its usual persistence.

"Hello, Frank?"

"Jerry? Is that you?"

"Yeah. Can I talk to you for a minute?"

"Sure. What's up?"

"Well, I know it's late and everything, but I really need to talk to you about something . . . ."

Frank braces for what's coming next.

"Frank, if somebody calls and asks you where I was last weekend, just say I was with you, OK?"

"What?"

"Just say that you and I were . . , uh . . , just say we were hunting at the cabin."

"Jerry, what's going on? You want me to *lie* for you?"

Silence.

"Well, you see, there's this girl, and . . ."

Frank explodes, "*What*?! Does Ellen know?"

"I don't know. Probably. All I know is, her lawyer might call you, and . . ."

"Her *lawyer*?! Jerry, what in the world is going on with you guys?"

Silence.

"Come on, Frank! Don't lecture me! You know how things are. Ellen doesn't have a clue what I'm going through."

"But, Jer . . ."

"Look, I don't want to get into it with you right now. It's late and we're both tired. Just do this one thing for me, OK?"

Silence.

Frank tries again.

"Come on, Jer. I'm your brother. You can . . ."

Now Jerry explodes.

"No I *can't*, Frank! Why is it that whenever I ask you to do the least little thing for me, you give me nothing but hassle? Oh . . . forget it! Why should *you* care what happens to *me*? You've got your pretty little wife, your cushy little job, your . . ."

"That's *enough*, Jerry!"

Silence.

"Just forget it, Frank, OK?

Click.

Frank's wife rolls over and asks,

"Who was that, honey?"

"Jerry."

"What does he want this time?"

"Nothing. Go back to sleep. I'll tell you about it later."

Frank replaces the phone and reaches for the light. Another late-night phone call from Jerry. How many have there been this month? Ten? Twenty? He knows he won't get much sleep tonight. Sleep is the last thing on his mind after one of Jerry's phone calls. His thoughts wander in and out of focus as he stares up at the ceiling-fan.

"How can I get off this merry-go-round?"

Things used to be different. Sure, they always had their share of brotherly spats. All brothers do. But now it's different, more intense, more ruthless. Jerry blames him for every problem in his life. Miles apart, Frank wants to get closer to his brother, but he doesn't know how to anymore. Like a moth to a flame, he fears that the closer he gets, the more he'll get burned.

They used to be a team. Whenever Frank pitched, Jerry caught. Whenever Frank mowed, Jerry raked. Whenever Frank washed, Jerry dried. Whatever they did, they did it as a team.

Until Vietnam.

The words *still* strike terror, even after all these years. Frank wonders when the war will be over. Oh, the Vietnam war was officially over years ago, but the war it fueled, the war it ignited, the ugly *sibling* war—*that* war still rages out of control.

Maybe it was the draft. Maybe it all started when Jerry drew a low number in the lottery while Frank drew a number in the 300s. Was this the beginning of his hatred for him? Or did it begin much earlier?

Jerry enlisted in the army. Frank enrolled in college. Jerry went to boot camp. Frank went to summer orientation.

Boot camp was tough on Jerry. Separation from family and friends was difficult. Military life, with its strict rules and mind-numbing monotony taxed Jerry's spirit like nothing else he had ever done.

Until he burned his first village.

Until he killed his first teenager.

Only those who were there will ever fully understand. The horror. The humiliation. The shame. The guilt. The waste. Frank sat in air-conditioned classrooms while Jerry slogged through snake-infested jungles. Frank went to fraternity parties while Jerry buried buddies he barely knew. Frank married a wonderful girl while Jerry sat in a lonely bunker night after night.

Consequently the Jerry who came home from the war was not the same Jerry who left. He never really recovered from the experience. His friends tried to pick up with him where they left off, but they didn't get very far. Nobody, not even his closest high school buddies, could get through the concrete-and-barbed-wire fence he'd put up. Soon there was whispering. People made fun of his walk, his talk, his haircut, his clothes.

In response, Jerry did the only thing he could. He laid another row of bricks in the wall surrounding his heart.

The first month back he called up a girl he had always liked, surprised to learn that she was still single. They went out to a movie on a Friday night and co-signed a lease for an apartment within six weeks. To please their parents, they tied the knot in a church wedding.

But it did little to stave off the inevitable.

The bottom fell out and Jerry laid another layer of bricks into the wall.[1]

At first, Frank patiently listened to the war-stories, crude and vulgar though they were. His training in psychology had taught him the value of reflective listening. He tried as hard as he could to listen to the pain. The drinking, the swearing, the lying, the marital infidelities—he tried to put it all aside and be there for his brother.

But it was too much. Too many late-night phone calls. Too many drunken stupors. Too many bitter words. Frank just couldn't take it anymore. Jerry had too much bottled-up rage for any one person to handle alone—even a big brother who loved him dearly.[2]

THE STORY

Sibling rivalry is common in Scripture. Cain and Abel, Moses and Aaron, Amnon and Absalom, Martha and Mary, Peter and Andrew—these are just some of the better-known examples. One story in particular, however, towers over all of them: the story of Jacob and Esau, certainly one of the most honestly human tales in all of Scripture. Even those who read the Bible solely for its literary beauty (dismissing its theology) find it fascinating.[3]

Like all Bible stories, however, this one is designed to do much more than entertain or amuse. Yahweh's initial prophecy to Rebekah makes this crystal clear:

"Two nations are in your womb. Two peoples are divided within your belly. One will be stronger than the other. The older will serve the younger" (Gen. 25:23).[4]

At the outset we might ask why these lines appear at the beginning of this narrative. I think they're here to link this particular *story* to its larger salvation *history*. The opening prophecy to Rebekah sets the entire tone for the narrative which follows. It helps us to see the genetic link between the micro-conflict of Jacob-vs.-Esau and the macro-conflict of Israel-vs.-Edom. In fact, failure to understand this linkage makes it difficult for us to appreciate either the story or the broader background history in their entirety. In a profound way, Jacob and Esau *are* Israel and Edom, two proud peoples constantly at each other's throats, just like their namesakes.[5]

Because this is a bi-leveled narrative, the subtleties of each level and its connection to the other sometimes make it difficult for us to find a single, coherent focal point. Yet this design is deliberate, not accidental. Because the *story* and the *history* are designed to blend into each other, it's hard to see where one ends and the other begins. So we have problems sometimes when we try to put a few simple questions to this text: Who is the hero of this story? Who is the villain? What is the source of the conflict? How is it resolved?

Esau, for example, seems far too gullible to be a "villain," at least not in the technical sense of the term.[6] Yet what is he, if not the "bad guy?" Impetuous and impatient, he sells his birthright for a bowl of stew (Gen. 25:33). He marries foreign, Canaanite wives against the wishes of his parents, particularly his mother (Gen. 26:35; 28:9). In spite of his noxious behavior, he still expects to receive the blessing of the firstborn (Gen. 27:4). When he doesn't, his brother becomes a convenient scapegoat for his anger and overall lack of maturity (Gen. 27:41-46).

Esau comes across as an immature, impulsive, rather arrogant young man at the beginning of this story.[7]

Jacob, on the other hand, seems far too manipulative to be a "hero." Instead, he looks very much like what his name implies, a "heel-grabber."[8] The first time we see him he's gouging his brother out of his legal inheritance (Gen. 25:31). Then he participates in a shameful scheme to deceive his father and secure the birthright for himself (Gen. 27:18-29).[9] Later, while running away from Esau's wrath, he has a profound religious experience:

"How terrifying is this place! This is none other than the house of God! (*Beth-el*). This is the very gate of heaven!" (Gen. 28:17).

God graciously comes to him in a dream and burns a vision of his glory deep into his heart.

Yet note how selfishly he bargains for advantage in the "covenant" he proposes to make with this God:

> If God will be with me, and will keep me in this way that I go, and will give me bread to eat and clothing to wear so that I can come again to my father's house in peace, then Yahweh shall be my God (Gen. 28:20-21).

Quite an interesting set of preconditions for a liar and a cheat, wouldn't you say? Granted, this speech *can* be read as an embryonic indicator of a budding faith, and many do read it this way. More likely, however, it shows us an example of simple youthful arrogance. Certainly it is one of the few times in Scripture where a human being dares to dictate covenant terms to God. Compared to the usual pattern of covenant-making, this is highly unusual.[10]

Still, Jacob seems to be the protagonist of this story—if not the "good guy," at least the guy who eventually *tries* to be good. It is the job of Uncle Laban to turn this *potential* into hard *reality*. From the day they meet, Rebekah's brother drafts Jacob into a graduate course in "heel-grabbing"—and Jacob doesn't like it. Laban gives him repeated, hefty doses of his own medicine. He lies to him about his daughter, and gives him Leah instead of Rachel as his wife. For fourteen years he treats him more like an indentured servant than a son-in-law.

From a literary standpoint, the irony here is delicious. Jacob, the man who steals his brother's birthright, has his own *wife* stolen right out from under him. Jacob, the man who deceives his old, blind father, is *himself* deceived.[11]

Garry Wills tells a story of a modern-day "Jacob," an official who came to national prominence as Jimmy Carter's budget director in the mid-1970s. Do you remember the fast-talking, back-slapping banker from Atlanta who, in 1974, invested over a million dollars in a losing campaign for governor, then borrowed millions more to purchase controlling interest in the National Bank of Georgia? Then he loaned these same millions to the Carter presidential campaign—money he owned only on paper.

By 1977 he was deeply in debt. But salvation appeared when Carter offered him the post of budget director in his new administration. Perhaps he thought that accepting this position would simply erase his financial problems. That's when he met "Laban"— the U. S. Senate. When several senators finally investigated his finances and discovered the magnitude of his improprieties, they immediately expelled him from public office. "Laban" pulled the rug out from under Bert Lance so fast he never knew what hit him.[12]

JACOB'S STRUGGLE

As the narrative continues, Jacob eventually begins to wonder whether life back home, even life with Esau, might be preferable to life with Laban. Confrontation, with all its risks, begins to look preferable to exploitation.

So he decides to go home. He finagles a relatively honest, nonmanipulative agreement with Laban and successfully extracts himself from his uncle's control. But as he leaves Padan-Aram, the question begins to rise in his mind whether he will be able to do the same with Esau. Will Esau listen to him after what he did to him, after fourteen years of bad blood? Will reconciliation be possible? (Gen. 31:44-50).[13]

The episode in which the brothers meet, the "showdown" for which the narrator so carefully prepares us, is embedded in one of the most textured sections of the book of Genesis. Attention to this texture is necessary, again, if we genuinely want to understand the significance of the biblical doctrine of reconciliation.

RECONCILIATION WITH GOD

The narrator returns to the two-leveled approach with which he began. Jacob's second encounter with Esau is woven into his second encounter with God. Within this two-tiered format, in fact, we can trace five distinct stages in the reconciliation process.

First, in the divine-human encounter Jacob (1) meets a troupe of divine "messengers,"[14] then (2) responds with an exclamation of awe (Gen. 32:7), then (3) names the place of the encounter "the two camps,"[15] then (4) "wrestles" with a being more powerful than himself,[16] then (5) changes his name from *Jacob* ("heel-grabber") to *Israel* ("struggler with God") (Gen. 32:28).

RECONCILIATION WITH ESAU

Each of these elements is carefully reproduced in Jacob's second encounter with Esau: (1) Jacob encounters 400 "angels/messengers" from Esau, then (2) trembles in awe before Esau's power, then (3) divides his entourage into "two camps" before going into his brother's presence (Gen. 33:1-3; 32:7).

Here, however, the parallels start to change. In the encounter between Jacob and *God*, Jacob wrestles with an "angel."[17] Expecting to find something similar in the encounter with Esau, what we see instead is a "wrestling-match" between Jacob and *Esau* over who will forgive the other first! Esau graciously offers Jacob an expensive gift of livestock. Jacob politely refuses. Esau then "urges" him to accept it until Jacob finally takes it (Gen. 33:11). Quite unlike the angel-wrestling scene, yet very much like it, what we see here are two men who look less like bitter enemies than old friends arguing over who's going to pick up the restaurant check!

At the fifth and final stage, Jacob changes his name—and this represents the culmination of his spiritual transformation. He takes on a new name symbolizing a new change of heart. The *divine-human* encounter climaxes when "Jacob" becomes "Israel." Similarly, the *human-human* encounter climaxes when Israel builds an altar and calls it *El Elohe Israel* (Gen. 33:20), a phrase which literally means, "God, the God of the one who wrestles with God." This represents an important step by Jacob because this altar publicly *confirms* his reconciliation with Esau. It institutionalizes it. It declares to the world that all the old names and the old attitudes have been thrown away. They no longer describe the new reality between these two men.[18]

Israel is *Jacob* no longer. *Israel* doesn't bargain with God anymore, he wrestles with truth. *Israel* doesn't define himself as someone's "little brother" anymore, he steps out on faith with his own identity.

CONFLICT RESOLUTION

Earlier in this century, most social-science studies of families and their problems tended to focus on parent-child issues. Recent approaches, however, have begun to take the sibling bond more seriously.[19] Birth-order research (begun in the 1960s) and family systems research (begun in the 1970s) have paved the way for this new focus.[20] Theorists and therapists are slowly coming to understand that unresolved sibling conflict can also exercise a profound impact on human behavior, and needs to be addressed in the healing process.[21]

Yet the dynamics of sibling rivalry can be both complex and unique at the same time. Some of this conflict can be explained by genetics and birth-order. But nongenetic factors play a part as well. As any parent can attest, two children within the same family can be radically different from each other. These differences can be explained by several nongenetic factors: differing parent-child relationships, differing experiences within the sibling relationship, the impact of growing up with an individual very different from oneself, influences beyond the immediate family, and chance.[22]

We need to recognize, therefore, that unresolved sibling conflicts, just like unresolved parent-child conflicts, often carry over into our adult relationships, wreaking havoc and causing deep distress.

Jane Greer sees two sibling types in any given family. The *Supersibling* is the brother or sister who gives to the point of frustration. Supersiblings have a hard time saying "no." They struggle with how to formulate legitimate expectations of their brothers and sisters. They define "love" by seeing to it that they're always there to bail their siblings out whenever they need help, even though they secretly resent them for it. Frank is a good example of the *Supersibling*. Firstborn children, in fact, are particularly prone to becoming *Supersiblings*.[23]

Jerry, on the other hand, struggles with the problem of the *Invisible Sibling*. Failing to resolve his sibling conflict with Frank, he finds it extremely difficult to relate to anyone. Unable to dominate Frank, he unconsciously tries to dominate everyone else in his life. His marriage fails, his friendships evaporate, and his career never gets off the ground because he still can't see the depth of his problem. Jerry is the typical little brother who wants to win so bad, he's willing to pay any price—even acute loneliness. To heal this wound, he needs to face squarely the root of his problem and stop importing it blindly into every other relationship in his life.

The question is, how? How can he become aware of this subconscious drive to succeed at all costs? How can he resolve his conflicts with his brother? How can he finally come to terms with reality and accept himself for who he is?

Scripture is clear in its response to this question. Whenever siblings or anyone else in Scripture decide to turn their frustrations over to God, as Jacob does, God immediately gives them the strength to deal with their brothers and their sisters on a new plane. Whenever they refuse to allow God into the equation, however, the conflict remains unresolved, the frustrations build, and tragedy often results.

One need only read the story of Cain and Abel in Genesis 4:1-16 to see how this works.[24] In the parable of the prodigal son, however, the younger brother's decision to return to his father makes it possible for him to receive the strength he needs to deal with the jealousy in his older brother (Luke 15:11-32). The same goes for sisters. Jesus' message to Martha is intended to help her re-prioritize her life. Jesus makes it possible for Martha to learn to appreciate better the gifts of a "lazy" younger sister after Jesus praises Mary for her spiritual priorities and obedient character (Luke 10:38-42).[25]

In other words, Scripture insists on the necessity of God's involvement in the process of conflict resolution, including sibling conflict resolution. Reconciliation cannot occur on the horizontal plane without simultaneously occurring on the vertical plane. We cannot have one without the other. When God reaches down from heaven and touches Jacob on the thigh, this experience irrevocably changes Esau's brother. The "angel" could easily have killed him, but this would not have solved his problem with Esau. Nor would removing Esau from the picture have resolved it, either.

Hyper-horizontal and hyper-vertical approaches to reconciliation never work. The only solution is for the two brothers to sit down and hammer out some sort of covenant agreement *before God*. We do not know how God prepares Esau for this covenant, but we do know how he prepares Jacob. He appears to him in an initiatory dream and offers him a vision of the future. He leads him into fourteen years of "exile" to purge his soul of its "heel-grabbing," manipulative lifestyle. He touches him on the thigh and burns into his brain the truth that genuine servants of God are always known by their "limp." He changes his name from *Jacob* to *Israel* to reflect the reality of this divine encounter.

Then and only then does he lead him back into fellowship with his estranged brother.

What a marvelous story! Prior to the divine encounter, Jacob is a fearful, driven man. After it he is able to face the unknown. Prior to his encounter with God and man, Jacob is a man on the run, a man forced to decide between favored wives and hard-won possessions. Afterwards, he is a man at peace, choosing to spend his time and money on things that really matter. Now he is able to stare death itself in the face and walk away a free man. Now he can find the strength to enter the "house of God" (*Beth-el*), and once he's there, he finally finds the strength to engage, indeed, to wrestle with a God who accepts him as he really is, warts and all.

This is what Jerry needs. He needs to feel the hand of a living God in his life. He needs someone to explain that pain in his "hip." He needs to stop looking for heels to grab, stop fighting off imaginary enemies. He needs to stop cowering in fear before the invisible siblings in his life. He needs to realize that Frank is not, and never will be God. He needs to realize that life without the Lord is much, much worse than life without Frank. He needs to believe in and talk to and wrestle with a God who accepts him as he is.

The war is over, Jerry.

QUESTIONS FOR DISCUSSION

(1) How does Jerry view the world?
(2) How does Frank view it?
(3) Is Esau a true "villain"? Is Jacob a true "hero"?
(4) Why is *Jacob's* name changed to *Israel*?
(5) How is Jacob's conflict with God resolved?
(6) How is Jacob's conflict with Esau resolved?
(7) Why does Jacob name his altar *El Elohe Israel*?

ENDNOTES

[1]For further study, see Patricia Allen and Sandra Harmon, *Getting to "I Do"* (New York: William Morrow and Co., 1994).

[2]Kevin Leman discusses how difficult it is for firstborn children to let go in *Growing Up Firstborn: The Pressure and Privilege of Being Number One* (New York: Delacorte, 1989) pp. 80-114.

[3]See, for example, J. P. Fokkelman, "Genesis," in Robert Alter and Frank Kermode, *The Literary Guide to the Bible* (Cambridge: Harvard, 1987) pp. 45-47.

[4]Sharon Pace Jeansonne illuminates the story of Rebekah in *The Women of Genesis: From Sarah to Potiphar's Wife* (Philadelphia: Fortress, 1990). For further study from a critically anthropological point of view, see Naomi Steinberg, *Kinship and Marriage in Genesis: A Household Economics Perspective* (Minneapolis: Fortress, 1993) pp. 87-114.

[5]For further study, see Thomas W. Mann, *The Book of the Torah: The Narrative Integrity of the Pentateuch* (Atlanta: John Knox, 1988) pp. 51-52.

[6]See Robert Alter, *The Art of Biblical Narrative* (New York: Basic Books, 1981) pp. 94-96.

[7]This is the image of Esau preserved in Hebrews 12:16-17.

[8]The Hebrew name "Jacob" means "heel-grabber" (Genesis 25:26). A dynamically equivalent translation of this term might be something like "wheeler-dealer" or "trickster."

[9]Devorah Steinmetz explores the patriarchal stories along these lines in *From Father to Son: Kinship, Conflict, and Continuity in Genesis* (Louisville, KY: Westminster/John Knox, 1991).

[10]Moshe Weinfeld surveys the concept of covenant in *Theological Dictionary of the Old Testament*, vol. 2 (Grand Rapids: Eerdmans, 1975) pp. 253-279. William Dumbrell offers a theological discussion in *The Faith of Israel: Its Expression in the Books of the Old Testament* (Grand Rapids: Baker, 1988) pp. 34-39.

[11]Note the difference between the realistic portrait of Jacob in Genesis and the less unflattering portrayals of him in Hosea 12:1-6 and Matthew 8:11. Paul does something entirely new with the Jacob tradition in Romans 9:10-12.

[12]Garry Wills, *Lead Time* (Garden City: Doubleday, 1983) pp. 156-165 (originally published in the *New York Review of Books*, Sept 29, 1977).

[13]Michael Rion discusses several of the problems involved in ethical decision-making in *The Responsible Manager* (New York: Harper and Row, 1990).

[14]The word for "angel" and the word for "messenger" are the same word in Hebrew.

[15]This is the meaning of the Hebrew proper name "Mahanaim" in Genesis 32:2.

[16]The mysterious "angel-wrestling" scene in Genesis 32:22-32.

[17]Actually, he wrestles with a "man" (Genesis 32:24-25).

[18]On the importance of communal ritual to cement reconciliation between individuals, families and churches, see Robert Webber, *Signs of Wonder: The Phenomenon of Convergence in Modern Liturgical and Charismatic Churches* (Nashville: Abbott Martyn, 1992) pp. 116-130.

[19]Stephen Bank and Michael Kahn, *The Sibling Bond* (New York: Basic, 1983).

[20]Barbara Mathias, *Between Sisters: Secret Rivals, Intimate Friends* (New York: Delacorte Press, 1992) p. x.

[21]Jane Greer and Edward Myers, *Adult Sibling Rivalry: Understanding the Legacy of Childhood* (New York: Crown, 1992).

[22]Judy Dunn and Robert Plomin, *Separate Lives: Why Siblings Are So Different* (New York: Basic, 1990) p. 152.

[23]Kevin Leman, *Growing Up Firstborn*.

[24]Kevin Leman has an interesting chapter on the sibling rivalry between Cain and Abel in *Growing Up Firstborn*.

[25]Marge Green's *Martha, Martha!* is still a classic devotional study of this text (Abilene: Quality Printing, 1964).

ESTHER'S DECISION

(ESTHER 1:1-4:16)

"Mom . . . I think I'm pregnant."

The words swooped down on her like angry bees, swarming, stinging.

"What . . ?!"

She tried to swat them away, but they wouldn't leave her alone.

"Mom, I only *think* I'm pregnant. I'm not really sure."

No place to run, no place to hide.

"You only *think* you're pregnant!"

Dumbfounded, Betty just stared at her seventeen-year-old daughter.

"Pregnant? No! Not my daughter! It can't be!" Terrifying options raced through her mind like fleeting shadows.

Abortion? . . . No.

Adoption? . . . No.

Marriage? . . . .

Then came the counterattack, full-force.

"How could you do this to me? Why do you want to hurt me? What are my friends going to say? What will your father say? Why are you doing this to me?"

Jenny's revelation had achieved its desired effect. Betty's facial expression changed from shock to terror to anger. Suddenly aware of my presence, she shot a look my way that screamed *"Help me!"* and *"Stay out of this!"* at the same time.

Jenny just hung her head and cried.

Betty had asked if I would meet with the two of them and "talk some sense into that daughter of mine." I hadn't seen either of them in a long time, so I didn't know what to expect. After our greeting, Jenny sat as far away as possible, while Betty monopolized the conversation. Trying to listen to her, I couldn't help noticing Jenny out of the corner of my eye, twitching and fidgeting in obvious agitation. Something was really wrong.

Betty continued laying down the law, her voice rising with every sentence:

"Do you know where we found her last night? Throwing up in the school parking lot, that's where! Drunk as she could be! *My* daughter! *Drunk*! Can you believe that? And all her little friends, too! Well, the party's over, young lady! Things are going to change around here! Your *father* and I . . . ."

For some reason, the mention of "your *father* and I" seemed to be the trigger, the pretext Jenny was looking for to strike back at her mother. It was then that she blurted out the news she had been holding in for weeks.

Sam and Betty were a handsome couple. Everybody said so. They met while working for the same law firm, two struggling young attorneys fresh out of law school. Sam was good-looking in a rugged, down-home sort of way. Betty, though, was a knockout, an extremely attractive woman who looked like someone in the pages of a fashion magazine.

They were the "ideal" American couple.

During the first year of their marriage Betty dutifully stuck to her childhood tradition of going to worship every Sunday. Sam usually slept in. This lasted until the baby came. Then things changed. Betty began to miss more and more of the assemblies. She rationalized her absence by saying it was just too hard to get Jenny ready without waking Sam up. Besides, who likes to sit alone in church?

It was the move North, though, that really threw Betty off track. Sam was offered a position in a large Northeastern firm. Betty had misgivings about leaving the South, where she had lived all her life, but this was a promotion for Sam and a chance to move closer to his folks. Betty couldn't stand in his way, so they accepted the promotion and made the move. What could go wrong?

Everything.

For the first time in her life, Betty had no friends and had to make new ones. People at church didn't feel as "friendly" as the folks back home. Sam's family dropped in whenever they pleased, unannounced. She couldn't seem to lose the weight she had gained during her pregnancy. Folks teased her about her thick Southern accent. Being a mother was much harder than she had ever imagined.

Nothing seemed to go right for Betty.[1]

Trying to get her life back on track, Betty "came forward" and publicly asked for prayer one Easter Sunday, and our tiny congregation prayed with her and for her. It seemed to help, for a while.

But her change of heart was short-lived. Within a month, she sank back into her old habits. Something always seemed to get in her spiritual way. The people at church now went from "cold" to "rude." Sam's family demanded more and more of his time, especially on weekends and holidays, and she resented them for it. When conflicts arose, Sam always seemed to take their side against hers. With Jenny, Betty soon realized that Sam had no intention of fathering his daughter beyond the absolute bare minimum of food, shelter and clothing.[2]

I first met Betty in the foyer at church and we became friends right away. It's hard not to like her, she's so funny, full of life. I remember one of our earliest conversations because in it she promised to bring Jenny to Bible class. To my playful prodding, she laughed and said, "All right, all right! I'll bring her! I promise!"

The sad part is that little Jenny really loved coming to Bible class. Her teachers would tell me she loved the songs. She loved the Bible stories. She loved the special events, like Vacation Bible School and mission trips. She loved everything about going to church . . . when she was little.

One particular Sunday morning, when Sam was away on a business trip, Betty and I had a long talk, and I began to see the other side, the hidden side of their relationship. She talked about how desperately homesick she was, about how much she resented Sam's increasingly possessive family, about how much she hated having to raise Jenny "by herself." She even confessed her growing suspicions about what Sam did for relaxation on his business trips.

She felt trapped and alone.[3]

After Jenny started preschool, Betty thrashed around for a while until she landed a job she really liked. The atmosphere, the hours, the new friends, the new responsibilities—everything about her job instantly filled up the gaping void in her life. She plunged into it with gusto. This meant, of course, that she had to spend a lot of time away from Sam and especially Jenny, but the satisfaction of doing something she really liked for a change was so intoxicating, she didn't care. She began to carve out a new life for herself.

Work made the loneliness more bearable. Work opened up new opportunities. Work provided extra spending money. Before she knew it, work became the most important thing in her life.[4]

Like most teenagers, Jenny knew precisely how to manipulate her parents in order to get what she wanted. She knew precisely where they differed in their value systems, and she knew precisely how to take advantage of it. Jenny was not an evil child, just a determined one.

When she became old enough to date, Betty "suddenly" realized she had a problem on her hands. Jenny was wild. She became known at school as the girl who would go anywhere and try anything. And Betty didn't know what to do about it. No one at church knew how to help, because no one at church really knew them anymore. Betty had systematically cut herself off from the church. Instead, she had stubbornly chosen to invest her life elsewhere, and the result of that choice was beginning to bear its awful fruit.[5]

When Jenny finally dropped her bombshell ("Mom, I think I'm pregnant!"), Betty's life came to a dead stop. Everything which seemed so important to her—her career, her looks, her money, her possessions—none of it could help her now. The time had come to make a decision. A hard, painful decision. And she had no idea whether she had the spiritual resources to make it. She only knew it wouldn't go away.

The inevitability of its appearance was as real as the mascara now streaming down her daughter's face.

THE STORY

The story of Esther begins with, of all things, a beauty contest. King Ahasuerus of Persia commands Vashti, his favorite plaything, to present herself before the king and his friends in what looks to be an ancient version of the Miss Universe pageant. Vashti, however, "just says no" to the king and his drinking buddies, a startling response which takes everyone in this story completely by surprise. Thoroughly embarrassed by this turn of affairs, the king scurries frantically to recover his pride. Upon the advice of his courtiers, he decides to banish Vashti from his presence, then begin the laborious search for a new queen. Esther "auditions" for, and eventually becomes that queen.

A good subtitle for *Esther* might be *"A Tale of Two Cultures."* Much like Charles Dickens' classic novel *A Tale of Two Cities*, two cultures stand in stark contrast here. The dominant culture is that of the Persian aristocracy: rich, powerful, and arrogant. The culture upon which they've planted their feet consists of several conquered peoples, now beaten down and brutally assimilated into the Persian empire. The Jews are part of this empire, a downtrodden, suffering people still lamenting the loss of their king and their temple to the Babylonians.

Mordecai and Esther are Jewish refugees growing up in this oppressive world, thrown together by painful circumstances. Esther begins life as a war orphan, though fortunate enough to have been adopted by her first cousin, Mordecai, a fourth-generation diaspora Jew whose great-grandfather had gone to Babylon during the first conquest of Jerusalem (Jer. 29:1).

Like other Jewish accounts about the exile, *Esther* reveals few details about the heroine's early life.[6] Instead, the narrator is content to portray her as a strong, beautiful, rather naive young woman. Mordecai, by contrast, is briefly sketched for us as a shrewd, independent, combative Jew, a man fiercely proud of his heritage and faithfully devoted to his God.[7]

The major conflict in the story smolders and flares between Mordecai and Haman, a chief adviser to Ahasuerus. It is the worst kind of conflict, the kind which feeds on centuries of ethnic hatred, deeply rooted in raw tribal emotion, stubbornly resistant to the Word of God.[8] Haman descends from the ancient Amalekites. He hates the Jews because of what Samuel the Hebrew did to his ancestor, Agag.[9] Thus when Mordecai refuses to bow before him in the streets of Susa, all the old hatreds come to the surface. He becomes infuriated, angry enough to kill not just Mordecai, but every Jew in the Persian empire. Unaware of this conflict,

Ahasuerus allows Haman to plot a "final solution" to rid Persia of its "Jewish problem."[10]

The conflict with which we are concerned, however, is that which arises between the cousins themselves in response to this horror. Mordecai takes a hardbitten, prophetic stance against Haman, challenging him directly, refusing to bow down before him because of who he is and what he represents. Like Rosa Parks on that Birmingham bus in 1955, Mordecai refuses to give up his seat to a bigot. Instead he courageously cries out for justice, knowing very well that it may cost him his life.

Esther, however, decides to take a different approach to conflict resolution. At first, it looks like she's too out of touch with the real world to understand fully the threat Haman truly represents. At least, this is what Mordecai thinks. Like Betty, Esther lives in an exclusive world, a world of wealth and privilege, prosperity and leisure. Oriental harems in the ancient Near East were a very protected world. Yet this is where Esther spends her days. Mordecai's cousin is no longer the orphaned daughter of refugee immigrants. Esther has "made it." Esther is the queen of Persia, the mistress of the most opulent empire in the ancient world.

CONFLICT IN THE FAMILY

To put it poetically, Mordecai is mortified by what he sees in the "new" Esther. Running to tell her about Haman's plans, he becomes discouraged by her initial response, especially when she asks him to remove his mourning garb of sackcloth. This makes him extremely upset. He wants to confront Haman immediately by means of a high-profile, straight-ahead approach. Esther, on the other hand, wants him to "tone things down." Yes, she is "deeply distressed" by the news he has brought her, but she doesn't want Mordecai to overreact and thereby undermine her influence with the king. Judging by what comes next, Mordecai interprets this as timidity and fear on Esther's part.

Assuming he is in better touch with the problem than she is, he then "pulls rank" on his cousin and *commands* Esther to go to the king.

> Mordecai also gave him a copy of the written decree issued in
> Susa for their destruction, that he might show it to Esther and
> explain it to her, and *command* her to go to the king (Esth. 4:8).

Mordecai thinks this is the *only* way to stop Haman. He thinks
that his approach to conflict resolution is the only approach.
Underlying this conviction seems to be the unwritten assumption
that the only way to deal with the problem of conflict is to attack it
head-on.

Esther, however, like other female mediators in Scripture, is
extremely wary of the direct approach. She knows that no one can
go into the presence of the king without an invitation, and she
hasn't been invited for weeks. She probably suspects that it will do
no good to become the the next Vashti, whose strikingly direct
approach was famous throughout Persia for falling on its face.
Following the spirit of Abigail, the wise woman of Tekoa, and
Tamar, she therefore counsels caution and restraint.[11]

Mordecai will have none of it, so he confronts her for her "lack
of conviction." In one of the most passionate, eloquent speeches in
all of Scripture, he threatens her directly if she doesn't go to the
king right away:

> Don't think[12] of hiding from all the Jews in the king's palace.[13] If
> you stay silent now, relief and deliverance will arise for the Jews
> from another quarter, while you and your father's family will perish.
> Who knows whether you have come to the kingdom for such a time
> as this? (Esth. 4:13-14).

Certainly this is a stirring plea, but we need to be careful not to
take it out of context. We need to see that Esther's behavior, regardless of Mordecai's accusations, does not automatically mean that
she cares nothing for the kingdom. Nor does it imply that she is
some sort of a coward. One could well argue, in fact, that this
speech shows us as much (or more) about Mordecai as it does about
Esther.

At any rate, whether or not this plea is the catalyst for the action
which follows, Esther eventually does go to the king. But even after
she does get involved, notice that she still chooses to approach this
conflict in an indirect way. First she ensnares Haman by winning
his confidence. Then, much like Abigail in her mediation of the

Nabal-David conflict, she defuses this crisis in stages. We outlined these stages above as *responsibility*, *risk*, and *reason*. Esther follows this same basic pattern. First she moves the conflict onto her own turf, then she creates an atmosphere conducive to the achievement of her goals, then she finally closes her well-laid trap.

CONFLICT RESOLUTION

This story, therefore, can be read as a studied contrast between opposing approaches to reconciliation. On the one hand we have the *direct* approach, represented by Mordecai. On the other hand we have the *indirect* approach, represented by Esther. The subtle point of the story, from our perspective, is that the indirect approach is often a far more effective method for resolving conflict than the direct approach.[14]

Given the number of stories in Scripture where women so often play mediatorial roles, the question arises whether gender might somehow be a determining factor. Back in the 1970s, the vast majority of social scientists would probably have answered "No." Recent biological research on the brain, however, has seriously challenged these unisex theories. The "nature-nurture" pendulum has now swung away from "nurture" toward a new focus on "nature" among contemporary researchers. The physical sciences are uncovering more and more evidence that men and women think, act, and speak differently not just because of the way we're *psychologically* conditioned. Another factor to consider is the way we're *biologically* "wired."[15]

Jinx Melia speaks from the perspective of an American businesswoman. Constantly called upon to mediate conflicts and "cut deals" in the business world, Melia has come to the conclusion that many business people fail to understand the essential differences between men and women. She has investigated the biological as well as the psychological evidence thoroughly and has come to agree with the neurophysiologists as well as the social-psychologists that men and women, because we think and act so differently, simply cannot be expected to conduct business in the same way.

This is nowhere more obvious, according to Melia, than when businessmen and businesswomen approach the delicate matter of conflict resolution in a national or international business deal. Men tend to be more "bottom line" and direct in their negotiations, while women are much more interested in the relationships between the parties involved.

Melia thinks that businesswomen ought to be willing to live with the "bottom line" mentality in the business world because business is basically a "bottom line" profession. She also argues, however, that the unique ability of women to get to this bottom line by indirect rather than confrontational means is a managerial resource few businesses recognize fully and implement adequately. In a highly competitive global economy, where conflict is inevitable and conflict resolution increasingly difficult, she eloquently concludes that American companies need all the help they can get, and should take advantage of every resource at their disposal.[16]

The same might be said for any other complex social organization, including churches. In this area, however, *productive* change seems just as often to be perceived as a threat as it is a promise, and certainly needs to be managed thoughtfully, carefully and biblically.[17] Responding to attacks from both the left and right, the President of Abilene Christian University frames the religious gender issue this way:

> The real issue revolving around women is not their role in the assembly. A greater issue is how males treat females *all the time.* . . . It is unfortunate that our recent discussions have centered around the role of women in the assembly to the neglect of this other theme. One can be an advocate of the leadership of women in the assembly and still treat women in general . . . in a rather unchristian way.[18]

So if Esther had listened to Mordecai and tried to do things his way, the story of Esther might have turned out very differently than it does. But she doesn't, and she doesn't for a very good reason. One of the primary reasons why the book of *Esther* has been preserved in the Bible is to show us that discretion, wisdom, patience, and moderation are important qualities in mediators like Esther. I don't believe that they're inherently feminine qualities, though they sometimes look that way. Yes, Scripture is filled with stories about godly women who possess these characteristics, but men can practice them, too. Look at Jesus. Look at Barnabas. Look at Jonathan. In the final analysis, the conclusion seems obvious that these traits have less to do with gender than with Spirit.

Betty learned a great deal from Esther. Her conflict with Jenny was not unresolvable. It was her approach that was inadequate. Once Betty chose to employ Esther's subtle, indirect methods in her relationship to Jenny, the relationship changed and her family achieved reconciliation.

And oh yes, Sam was eventually baptized into Christ.[19]

QUESTIONS FOR DISCUSSION

(1) Compare and contrast the responses of Esther, Abigail, and Hannah to the conflicts in their lives.
(2) Do you know anyone like Esther? What do you most admire about her?
(3) Do you know any Mordecais? Describe.
(4) Do you think Mordecai ever came to appreciate Esther's wisdom?
(5) How are Betty and Esther similar? How are they different?
(6) When is it appropriate to use *direct* methods for resolving conflict?
(7) When is it more appropriate to use *indirect* methods?

ENDNOTES

[1]See Georgia Witkin-Lanoil, *The Female Stress Syndrome* (New York: Berkley, 1984).

[2]John W. Miller discusses the desperate need for father-involved families in *Biblical Faith and Fathering: Why We Call God "Father"* (New York: Paulist, 1989).

[3]Edward A. Charlesworth and Ronald G. Nathan list several "irrational" beliefs which combine to inhibit personal growth in their book *Stress Management: A Comprehensive Guide to Wellness* (New York: Atheneum, 1984) pp. 222-225.

[4]Juliet Schor convincingly argues that too many Americans, particularly American women, are stressed-out from overwork in *The Overworked American* (New York: Basic Books, 1992). For an alternative view, see Chuck Colson and Jack Eckerd, *Why America Doesn't Work* (Dallas: Word, 1991).

[5]"Adolescents exhibit the process of growing up into adulthood in a particularly vivid form. Their parents are unavoidably involved in it. Every parent of an adolescent is thus provided with a gift—a kind of living laboratory in which to take the data of growing up, work experiments with it in personal ways, and then reexperience it in an act of faith to the glory of God. Parents don't always look at it this way. Not infrequently, they are heard to complain about it. Many stoically stick it out, assured by the experts that adolescence is self-curing and will be over in seven or eight years. They never open the gift; they never enter the laboratory. But adolescence is a gift, God's gift, and it must not be squandered in complaints or stoic resistance." See Eugene Peterson, *Growing Up With Your Teenager* (Old Tappan, NJ: Revell, 1987) pp. 12-13.

[6]See the books of *Judith* and *Tobit* in the Apocrypha (the fifteen books accepted by Roman Catholics as Scripture, but by Protestants only as, at best, history).

[7]The word "God," however, does not appear in the book of Esther.

[8]See Hunter Lewis, *A Question of Values* (San Francisco: Harper, 1990) pp. 86-93. For "new world" parallels, see Thomas V. Peterson, *Ham and Japheth: The Mythic World of Whites in the Antebellum South* (Metuchen, NJ: Scarecrow, 1978).

[9]Agag is the Amalekite king whom Samuel "hacks to pieces before the Lord" in 1 Samuel 15:7-9.

[10]Much like Hitler's plan to annihilate the Jews in the 1930s.

[11]See 1 Samuel 25, 2 Samuel 14, and Genesis 38. For further study, see M. S. Moore, "Wise Women or Wisdom Woman? A Biblical Study of Women's Roles," *Restoration Quarterly* 35 (1993) pp. 147-158.

[12]Literally, "don't fantasize in your soul."

[13]An early translation of this Hebrew line into Greek reads "Don't say to yourself, 'I alone will be saved in the kingdom among all the Jews'."

[14]One way to explain the difference is to see Mordecai representing a *prophetic* approach, while Esther represents a *wisdom* approach to conflict resolution. Important distinctions between these complementary Israelite groups can be found in William McKane, *Prophets and Wise Men* (London: SCM, 1965).

[15]See Judy Dunn and Robert Plomin, *Separate Lives: Why Siblings Are So Different* (New York: Basic, 1990); and the important article, citing several sources, by Christine Gorman, "Sizing Up the Sexes," *Time* 139, 3 (Jan 20, 1992) pp. 42-51.

[16]Jinx Melia, *Breaking Into the Boardroom: What Every Woman Needs to Know* (New York: G. P. Putnam's Sons, 1986). See also Tara Roth Madden, *Women vs. Women: The Uncivil Business War* (New York: The American Management Association, 1987); Ann M. Morrison et al., *Breaking the Glass Ceiling* (Reading, MA: Addison-Wesley, 1987).

[17]See the important book by Lynn Anderson, *Navigating the Winds of Change: How to Manage Change in the Church* (West Monroe, LA: Howard, 1994).

[18]Royce Money, "On This Rock" (A speech delivered to the Abilene Christian University Bible Lectureship, February 21, 1993). For further study, see Bonnidell and Robert G. Clouse, eds., *Women in Ministry: Four Views* (Downers Grove, IL: InterVarsity, 1989).

[19]After I performed Jenny's marriage ceremony, mother, daughter and granddaughter were all in Bible class the Sunday after the baby was born. Betty successfully established a behavior pattern which Sam found irresistible, and eventually, after several years of faithful obedience, led to Sam's conversion and the joyful reuniting of his family in Christ.

SAMSON'S FEAR

(JUDGES 13:1-16:31)

Lisa's voice was quiet, but determined.

"I think we should see other people . . . ."

What?

"I know this is painful for you . . . ."

What? How could she even *think* this way?

"I just don't think we're right for each other."

Mark felt like he had been shot in the chest. Unable to meet her gaze any longer, his eyes fell helplessly to the ground. Across the quadrangle, he could see several other couples saying goodnight, their tender embraces frozen in time.

"But, don't you *love* me?"

His lips trembled. His eyes misted up.

"We'll always be friends, Mark. But I think we should, you know . . . . I think we should . . . stop dating. I'm sorry . . . ."

No! This can't be happening! After all that they had been through together? How could this be happening? *She said she loved me!*

"Lisa, wait . . . ."

"Goodbye, Mark."

And just like that, she was gone. Already on the stairs to her dormitory room. Already on the way out of his life.

Stunned, devastated, he could only shake his head in disbelief. Falling into a swing on the quadrangle, he tried to figure out what had happened. What had gone wrong? She was supposed to be "the one." Had she forgotten the promises they had made? Could it all have been a dream? *How could I have been so wrong?*

Connell Cowan and Melvyn Kinder describe the feeling well.

"These emotions have origins as deep as a child's first emotional connection. Romance can be exquisitely painful."[1]

99

Romance. Everyone wants it. Few ever find it. Fewer still ever see it ripen into mature love. Mark felt he had found it with Lisa. Young college sophomores with their whole lives ahead of them, the two of them "fell in love" on a summer mission trip. Mutual friends had told them about the campaign meetings on campus, how motivational they were, how inspirational. Impressionable and eager, they separately attended a Thursday night meeting in the Bible building, and immediately got caught up in the excitement.

Brazil. The very word sounds romantic. Every Thursday night they learned more about the people, the culture, the language, the Lord's work in Brazil. They oohed and aahed at the slides of Rio de Janeiro. Veteran campaigners stopped by to give glowing testimonies of earlier missions. Their mouths dropped along with everyone else's at the dramatic photos of the Christ statue, the trademark icon high above the city of Rio, its arms spread wide over the country like a "mother over her brood" (Matt. 23:37).

Arriving in Sao Paulo, they learned a lot about missions that summer. They sang the Gospel in churches and town-squares. They folded innumerable pieces of Christian literature. They knocked on hundreds of doors. They listened to scores of sermons they couldn't understand. Parroting door-to-door invitations in hilariously broken Portuguese, they delighted every Brazilian who took the time to listen.

The first week someone paired them to work together, and this proved to be a fateful decision. For the next six weeks they plunged headlong into the work (and one another) with boundless enthusiasm. That's when they saw the darker side of campaigning. Unpaved streets. Dead pedestrians on the sidewalk, covered with newspaper. Mounds of refuse. Open sewage. Vicious watchdogs. They inhaled some of the most rancid odors imaginable. They even ate *feijoada*, the rice-and-beans staple of the Brazilian diet, and got sick together when their American stomachs disagreed with it.

They did much good that summer. Evangelistic campaigns can change lives. *God Be With You 'til We Meet Again* takes on a whole new meaning when sung to a weeping church in a crowded airport. International missions provide perspective. They help future missionaries make important decisions about their life's work. They motivate young people to realign their spiritual priorities. Some students have even been known to change their major field of study after coming home from a campaign.

But the excitement they generate can sometimes be a little *too* intoxicating. It's hard to keep your mind on your mission when you're floating hand-in-hand over the beautiful cobblestoned streets of a sixteenth-century village with a willing young co-ed. It's hard to concentrate on the Lord when you're trekking the beaches of a famous international resort, barefoot and carefree. The lights of Rio at night can dazzle and seduce even the staunchest soul into forgetting, for a moment, the original reason for the mission.

That's exactly what happened to Mark and Lisa. Brazil became a dreamland. Reality turned into something long ago and far away. Past and future no longer existed, only present. Infatuation hit these kids like a freight train in high gear. Small talk led to mutual interests. Mutual interests led to mutual desires. Mutual desires led to . . . well, *deeper* mutual desires.

Their romance blossomed like a fragile orchid.

But take an orchid out of its protective environment, and it soon dies. The same is true for romance. Infatuation is too often confused with love anyway, but oh, how murky things can be when nobody but the person sitting next to you can speak a word of English.

THE STORY

In the Bible, Scripture has little to say about romance. When it does speak about it, however, it speaks with power and clarity. Read the *Song of Songs*. In these lushly erotic love songs, romance is real and precious and vital to human sexual relationship.[2] Eugene Peterson points out that the *Song*

> acknowledges the difficulty and the pain of the quest (for intimacy) and shares it. It does not attribute the agony of longing to a neurosis, it does not search for a cause in moral deficiency, it does not try to 'cure' it by working for an adaptive adjustment to 'reality.' It honors the quest.[3]

Covenant, however, transcends romance in the Bible and regulates it for the good of the community in God's Creation.[4]

"Covenant . . . means that humanity cannot understand life apart from a defined and revealed relationship with God. Before anything else, we are part of an arrangement—a relationship."[5]

Covenant transcends romance because covenant reflects the very image of God. Since God is not solitary, neither are we. God is Father, Son and Holy Spirit. Likewise human beings are male and female, separate genders united together in "one flesh" via covenant.[6] Any biblical theology worthy of its salt will always affirm that God created male and female to live in covenant.[7]

However, because romance is so individualized today, so cut off from all discussion of morality and ethics, this is a "hard saying" for many. Comprehension of it is made even more difficult by the format in which the Bible presents it. Most Scriptural teaching on love and romance comes to us in the form of non-narrative material —like the Song of Songs. Jesus' words on marriage, for example, are rarely found in his parables. The same is true for the preserved writings of Paul and Peter. (See Matt. 19:1-12; 1 Cor. 7:1-40; 1 Pet. 3:1-7.) For a culture like ours, where story-telling is *the* primary means of communication, this format presents a major obstacle to communication.

Consequently ministers of reconciliation have at least two barriers to overcome. The *content* of Scriptural teaching on marriage and romance is difficult enough to access and understand. But the *form* in which it is housed is becoming foreign as well to the people in the churches where we live and serve.[8]

The story of Samson, however, is an exception to this general rule. In fact, Judges 13-16 is a rare thing in Scripture, an actual *story* about marriage. Actually, the story of Samson is a story about several male-female relationships. The main character, Samson, is a boy/man forever "falling in love" with women, yet never really learning how to live in covenant with any woman. His intentions are noble, but his actions consistently belie his intentions. He does not know how to keep from being manipulated by women. He does not know how to satisfy a woman's emotional needs. Apparently he will not make himself vulnerable to one long enough to find out what they are.

Why?

SAMSON AND HIS PARENTS

Not much is told us about Samson's relationship to his parents, but from what little we know, it doesn't look healthy.

First, Samson is a Nazirite, a man "vowed" to God in a special way.[9] At the beginning of the narrative, Yahweh's angel delivers explicit instructions to his mother about his Nazirite future and urges her to take them seriously (Judg. 13:3-7). Like better-known Hannah (1 Sam 1:21-28) and Elizabeth (Luke 1:5-80), she faithfully obeys and commits to raising her son as a Nazirite, even though she knows this will be a difficult task:

> I raised up some of your sons for prophets, and some of your young men for Nazirites . . . but you made the Nazirites drink wine, and commanded the prophets saying, "You shall not prophesy!" (Amos 2:11-12).

Her good intentions, however, never quite translate into actual reality. Samson fights her every step of the way. According to the Mosaic law, Nazirites are supposed to observe three basic restrictions: no alcohol, no defilement (no touching of anything dead), and no haircuts (Num. 6:1-21). Samson's parents make every effort to comply with these restrictions.

But Samson refuses to cooperate. Instead, as the narrative makes clear, he stubbornly violates all three of these vows.

First, on the road to Timnah, he kills a lion. Then, returning home, he sees a swarm of bees building a honeycomb in the animal's carcass. A true Nazirite would turn away immediately from this temptation to defilement, but not Samson. Instead, he actually scrapes out the honey from the animal's corpse and eats it. A more graphic violation of the Nazirite vow would be hard to imagine (Judg. 14:5-9).

Second, at Timnah he throws a feast to celebrate his upcoming marriage—a "bachelor party," if you will. The word used to describe this "feast" seems significant. Hebrew narrators have a number of synonyms for "feast" at their disposal, yet the word chosen here is the noun form of the verb "to drink," a term usually associated with drunkenness and carousing (Esth. 5:6; Dan. 1:5). Thus, by describing Samson's "feast" by this means, the narrator leaves little doubt in our minds that Samson probably drank alcohol at Timnah, and if he did, this would be a further violation of his Nazirite vows (Judg. 14:10).

The third vow falls when he allows Delilah to give him a haircut. Now one could certainly argue that Delilah ought to take her share of the blame for this violation, just as the Timnite woman ought to be held partially responsible for the events which lead up to the Lehi incident (Judg. 15:14-17). But regardless of Delilah's behavior, when Samson violates this third restriction his fall becomes complete and the tragic flaw in his character becomes fully revealed (Judg. 16:19).

In other words, the narrator wants us to see a Samson who does everything he can to offend, embarrass and humiliate his parents. Although he tries valiantly to put as positive a twist on this behavior as he can, the truly amazing thing about Samson is that Yahweh uses him *in spite of* his behavior, not *because of* it. We need only contrast his actions with that of several other leaders in the period of the judges to realize this; consider, for example, Gideon, Deborah, and Samuel.

Moreover, Samson tries to keep the truth about these violations away from his parents. I don't believe he set out to lie overtly. He simply does what all adolescents do, sooner or later. He withholds the truth from his parents. He kills a lion on the way to Timnah, but covers it up (Judg. 14:6). He brings home honey from its rotting carcass, but doesn't say where he found it (Judg. 14:9). He plunges headlong into a romantic liaison with a foreign, Philistine woman, but fails to mention anything about it until marriage becomes imminent and his parents have to know (Judg. 14:3).

Evidently Samson has a hard time communicating with his parents.

SAMSON AND THE TIMNITE WOMAN

As Robert Alter has pointed out, men often romance their wives in Scripture by means of a conventional pattern. Isaac and Rebekah, Jacob and Rachel, Moses and Zipporah, Boaz and Ruth—each of these stories fits a customary pattern. The usual elements include (a) the journey of a husband to a foreign land, (b) a meeting at a well, (c) the drawing of water at this well, and (d) an invitation to dine at the home of the bride-to-be's parents. Alter calls this pattern the "betrothal type-scene."[10]

Reflecting the volatility of his troubled life, Samson deliberately violates each one of these romantic conventions. His courtship of the Timnah woman is little more than a sarcastic parody on the "typical" Hebrew romance. Notice. Samson (a) travels to foreign soil all right, but he doesn't stay there. Instead, he shuttles back and forth between his parents and his in-laws. In place of (b) a well and (c) the "water-drawing" scene, we see (b) a dead lion and (c) the "drawing" of honey from its defiled carcass. Finally, instead of (d) a cordial meal at the home of *her* parents, we hear a presumptuous command from Samson to *his* parents:

"Get her for me as wife" (Judg. 14:3).

In short, Samson is a tragic figure. The supreme irony of this narrative is that the strongest man who ever lived never makes it out of emotional adolescence. Like Achilles in Greek myth, Samson is a hero with a fatal flaw, an "Achilles heel." Like David, this flaw manipulates and subverts his romantic life. Unlike David, however, he never decides to deal with it seriously, even when it threatens to destroy him.

The first test of his marriage to the Timnite woman (who is never named, by the way) comes in the form of pressure from the Philistines—the "in-laws." Samson tells them a riddle at his bachelor party and dares them to figure it out. When they can't, they go to his *fiancée* and press her to tell them the secret of the riddle. Why? Because they're afraid that they may have to suffer embarrassment at the hands of this Hebrew. So afraid are they, in fact, they actually threaten her with violence and pain if she doesn't comply.[11]

So she does what many spouses do when confronted with a conflict. She transfers their anger straight to Samson:

"You only hate me! You don't love me! You have put a riddle to my countrymen, and you haven't told me what it is!" (Judg. 14:16a).

Samson's response, however, is just as reprehensible. He treats her with contempt and disrespect. He treats his wife the same way he treats his mother. He dismisses her. He makes no attempt even to listen to her, much less empathize with the pressure she's under. This is implied by his curt response:

"Look. I haven't told my father or my mother. And shall I tell you?" (Judg. 14:16b).

For seven days she nags him about this stupid riddle until finally he gives in just to shut her up. Here, then, is the classically dysfunctional marriage. She nags, he ignores. She pressures, he withdraws. Marriage counselors are very familiar with this pattern. It's as common as water today, as pervasive as the air we breathe.[12]

The second test comes when Samson tries to patch things up. Having lost face to the Philistines, he murders thirty men in a nearby town and gives their clothes to his in-laws. Angry and humiliated, he then slinks back to his parents' house. His father-in-law, thinking that the marriage is over, understandably gives his daughter to another man.

But when Samson has a change of heart and returns later to claim his spouse, he discovers that she's been given to someone else. Incredibly, he thinks he can offer a *goat* to his father-in-law as payment for the mayhem he has already caused. Then, when he discovers that his wife has been given to another man, the "wheels come off" and Samson goes totally berserk, killing not thirty men this time, but a thousand men with the jawbone of an ass (Judg. 15:1-16).

Why? Why does he become so unpredictably violent?

Several years ago, when my brother was a young police officer, he thought it would be fun to take me out with him on patrol one New Year's Eve. Obtaining permission for me to ride with him in his squad car, the two of us cruised Norfolk, Virginia into the wee hours of New Year's day. The only thing that frightened me more than his driving was the domestic dispute call we received at about 1:00 AM. Squawking and cracking, the dispatcher's voice came over the radio to tell us that a man was beating his wife in a nearby apartment complex.

Rushing to the address, I stayed downstairs with the wife and kids while my brother and another officer bravely went upstairs. The man was drunk and he had a gun and it was scary. Eventually my brother and his partner persuaded him to sit down and sober up, but not until two cops, one wife, two kids, and one minister had been scared half to death! I have since learned that police officers always dread such calls because they have found that domestic conflict is always the most unpredictably violent.

SAMSON AND DELILAH

Several years ago the news broke that the U. S. Embassy in Moscow had been the target of a successful plan to infiltrate our national defenses. The Soviets stole some of our most sensitive secrets. No one knew exactly how much information was pilfered, but the damage was thought to be incalculable. One version of the story claimed that two Marine guards had succumbed to the sexual advances of a female KGB agent.

The American public was outraged. The word on the street was, "How could a U. S. Marine sell out his country for sex?" Politicians and various media types pontificated for days about it. Ethics suddenly became the "hot button" issue on the nightly news. "Experts" of all sorts were called in. Telephone banks lit up on radio stations and TV talk shows for days.

Only a few, however, dared to ask the deeper question about this incident: How can a society unable to control its sexual lusts expect *not* to be attacked via illicit, mindless, commitment-less sexual lust?

Delilah was the Philistines' "KGB agent." When the Philistines realized that Samson had a weakness— women—the word went out and they immediately hired the latest of his Philistine lovers to deceive him. Delilah, Samson's final attempt at a romantic relationship, proved to be amazingly effective as an agent for the enemy. Her motivation was different, but her espionage technique was practically a carbon-copy of the Timnite woman's: make friends with the target, entice him, get him addicted to sex, then manipulate him ruthlessly.[13]

First, she politely asks him to tell her the secret of his superhuman strength. Samson responds just as politely: he lies to her. Then she tries again, accusing him of mocking her. Again Samson lies. Finally, she abandons all civility and *demands* that he tell her the truth, only to be rebuffed a third time by another lie.

Undaunted, she then simply rolls out the same emotional artillery that the Timnite woman had used so effectively years earlier.

"How can you say 'I *love* you' when your heart is not with me? You have mocked me these three times! You have not told me the secret of your great strength!" (Judg. 16:15).

Poor Samson. All Delilah has to mention is the "*L*-word," and instantly he turns to putty in her hands. This man is as insecure in this relationship as in all the ones preceding. He still doesn't know the meaning of "love." In fact, he prefers to have his "soul vexed to death" rather than face his deep inner conflict over the meaning of "love" (Judg. 16:16). Extortion is the only way a woman can get through to him.

CONFLICT RESOLUTION

The Screwtape Letters is C. S. Lewis' well-known, chillingly accurate portrait of the devil's character and mission. One of these letters has an older demon named "Screwtape" giving diabolical advice to his protégé, a younger demon named "Wormwood." In it, he teaches his protégé about the foibles and flaws of human nature, and advises him as follows:

> Avail yourself of the ambiguity in the word "love." Let them think they have solved by "love" problems they have in fact waived or postponed under the influence of the enchantment. While it lasts, you have your chance to foment the problems in secret, and render them chronic.[14]

How insightful. How tragically true. For most of the human race, "love" is a notoriously ambiguous word. Since defining it is quite difficult, the devil knows that he can make it even more ambiguous if he can make us—his prey—try to define it apart from the reality of God and God's covenant-making character.

Lewis is not alone in his analysis.

Willard F. Harley has pondered deeply what it means to "fall in love." A seasoned marriage counselor, Harley believes that most people are intensely interested in finding a "significant other" to meet *their* needs, yet very few seem willing to learn how to meet the needs of others. After twenty thousand clients, he develops what he calls a "need index" and presents it in a book called *His Needs, Her Needs*. His needs are (in order) sexual fulfillment, recreational companionship and an attractive spouse. *Her* needs are (in order) affection, conversation, and honesty. Harley concludes that:

as long as we fail to see marriage as a complex relationship that requires special training and abilities to meet the needs of . . . the opposite sex, we will continue to see a discouraging and devastating divorce rate.[15]

Jordan and Margaret Paul go a step further. This married professional couple warn that people can become so desperate for "love" they sometimes go to almost unbelievable extremes, even to the point of compromising their emotional, spiritual and sexual identities. They say that this is terribly common today, and terribly unhealthy. They argue that the goal of a healthy romantic relationship is to nurture individual freedom and integrity, but within the context of genuine, loving intimacy. Unhealthy relationships are comprised of partners who threaten and demand, withdrawing their "love" if they don't get their way.

The Pauls (and every other therapist I've ever read) believe that conflict is inevitable. They also believe that all responses to conflict proceed from one of two basic intentions: a desire to *protect* or a desire to *learn*. Couples in which one or more of the partners live in a constant state of *protection* never achieve real intimacy. Like Samson, there's too much fear there, too much uncertainty. Only those who dare to see conflict as an opportunity to *learn* something about themselves develop the strength to overcome their fears, rekindle romance, and discover intimacy.[16]

The evidence from both Scripture and the arena of secular psychotherapy seems clear. Love is not something one "falls into." Love is something one *decides*.[17] Love is not infatuation. Love is something which is tough, resilient, and adult. It is not something practiced well by adolescents, whatever their chronological age.[18] The story of Samson is consequently much more than the biblical equivalent of the Hercules myth. Perhaps a primary reason for its preservation is to show us precisely what our selfish adolescent selves, left unredeemed, can *really* do to those precious few people in our lives whom we say we "love."

For an age like ours, filled with millions of lonely people, all struggling to find romance, all struggling to define "love," it's hard to imagine a more relevant message.

QUESTIONS FOR DISCUSSION

(1) Describe what a failed romance feels like.
(2) What is a Nazirite? Is Samson a true Nazirite?
(3) Why does Samson treat his parents the way he does?
(4) What are the elements of a "typical" Hebrew romance?
(5) How well does Samson communicate with women?
(6) Why does Samson lie to Delilah?
(7) Why has the story of Samson been preserved in Scripture?

ENDNOTES

[1]Connell Cowan and Melvyn Kinder, *Smart Women, Foolish Choices* (New York: Clarkson N. Potter, 1985) p. 89.

[2]For further study, see Joseph C. Dillow, *Solomon on Sex: The Biblical Guide to Married Love* (Nashville: Thomas Nelson, 1977).

[3]Eugene Peterson, *Five Smooth Stones for Pastoral Work* (Atlanta: John Knox, 1980) pp. 46-47.

[4]Thomas Aquinas sees the marriage covenant as a sign pointing directly toward humanity's covenant with God through faith. Walter Kaspar discusses the implications of Aquinas' thinking in his book, *Theology of Christian Marriage* (New York: Crossroad, 1989) p. 8.

[5]Peterson, *Five Smooth Stones*, p. 42.

[6]See Karl Barth, *Church Dogmatics* (translated by J. W. Edwards, O. Busscy and Harold Knight; Edinburgh: T. and T. Clark, 1958) vol. III, part 1, paragraph 41, sections 2-3.

[7]Brevard Childs offers a groundbreaking new biblical theology in his *Biblical Theology of the Old and New Testaments: Theological Reflection on the Christian Bible* (Minneapolis: Fortress, 1992). Note especially pp. 658-716, "The Shape of the Obedient Life: Ethics."

[8]Neil Postman reflects on our culture's growing preoccupation with *story* in *Amusing Ourselves to Death: Public Discourse in an Age of Show Business* (New York: Viking, 1985).

[9]"Nazirite" comes from a Hebrew word for "to vow."

[10]Robert Alter, *The Art of Biblical Narrative* (New York: Basic, 1980) pp. 47-62.

[11]Riddle-telling is more than just a form of entertainment. It is also an ancient means of empowerment. The telling of riddles demonstrated intellectual prowess over one's enemies through the use of satirical double-meaning and innuendo. James Crenshaw discusses Samson's riddle in *Samson: A Secret Betrayed, A Vow Ignored* (Atlanta: John Knox, 1978) pp. 99-120.

[12]Nancy Good discusses this pattern at length in *How To Love a Difficult Man* (New York: St. Martin's, 1987).

[13]The Timnite woman is motivated by *fear* to wear Samson down. Delilah appears to be motivated by *greed*.

[14]C. S. Lewis, *The Screwtape Letters* (Chicago: Lord and King Associates, 1976) p. 121.

[15]Willard F. Harley, Jr., *His Needs, Her Needs* (Old Tappan, NJ: Revell, 1986) p. 175. A critical review of Harley appears in *Christian Studies* 10 (1989) pp. 64-66.

[16]Jordan and Margaret Paul, *Do I Have To Give Up Me To Be Loved By You?* (Minneapolis: CompCare, 1983) pp. 1-19.

[17]Gary Smalley, *Love Is A Decision* (Dallas: Word, 1989).

[18]James Dobson, *Love Must Be Tough* (Dallas: Word, 1983).

HANNAH'S BARRENNESS

(1 SAMUEL 1:1-18)

The words fell out of her mouth and hit me like a sledgehammer. "John and I are getting a divorce." I couldn't believe it. Two of my best friends in all the world were throwing away their marriage like a piece of trash, and I stood utterly powerless before it. I asked, "Why? How could this happen?"

She said, "I deserve to be *happy*, don't I?" Then she said, "I just don't love him anymore," and walked away.

For years the four of us had been inseparable. We did practically everything together. Friday nights at the movies. Tennis on Saturdays. Sunday afternoon dinners. Summer vacations at the shore. Countless discussions on every conceivable topic: music, sports, religion, politics, God, astronomy, the Bible, the church, the afterlife, the corporate business world.

Ours was one of those rare friendships where everyone laughs at the joke before the person telling it can get to the punch line.

One summer we took a canoe trip together. The water level in the river was low, as I recall, so we had to pick up our canoes a few times and carry them over the dry spots. This usually provoked a good deal of griping and complaining, especially among the men of the expedition. But no one really minded. The extra work just gave us an excuse to work up a heartier appetite.

John would often say, "There are two things in this world I won't eat: coconut and barbed wire."

I never saw him eat either.

As lunchtime grew closer on the river, a small island came into view where we beached the canoes for a while and relaxed. We had prepared a picnic lunch, and it turned out to be a memorable one. We feasted like royalty on tuna-fish sandwiches, deviled eggs, shrimp cocktail, raw vegetables, and pastries for dessert. Everything was perfect. Blue sky. Gentle breeze. Lazy river. Good friends. Other canoers paddling by, yelling, "What's for lunch?!"

Now it was coming to an end because . . . well, because "we just aren't *happy*."

The first time I saw Jennifer she was a shy young woman hiding in the back of the auditorium during one of my sermons. Someone told me she had grown up in the church all her life, but having married a non-Christian, she evidently felt awkward coming to worship by herself. Yet there she was, as close to the back of the building as possible, carefully positioning herself during the final song to bolt for the parking lot before anyone could actually speak to her.

It wasn't long, though, before she began to warm up to the congregation. All it took was a little love and affection, and she began to come out of her shell, take a deep breath, and accept God's grace. She began to participate not only in the assemblies, but also in the special events of the Family, like church picnics and fellowship dinners. She volunteered to keep teenagers overnight for youth events and participated in a weekly Bible study in the home of one of the elders. John and I played tennis constantly, practically every weekend. John and Jennifer even vacationed with other couples in the congregation, so close were they becoming to other Christians in the Family.

Both seemed to be growing spiritually, and all of us had high hopes that John would soon become a Christian.

But there was a problem. John and Jennifer could not have a baby. The pain of barrenness cast a dark cloud over their relationship. They never discussed it openly, but some of us began to notice that Jennifer seemed to be volunteering for nursery duty a lot. Little children, especially babies, became an obsession with her. She had one in her arms constantly. At one church picnic, for example, I remember seeing her with a flock of children around her for hours, reading to them and playing with them most of the day while their parents ate hamburgers and played softball and pitched horseshoes.

Few of us knew exactly why they could not have children of their own. It was a painful subject, and neither of them ever really talked about it openly. Looking back on the tragedy, I am persuaded that the barrenness itself was painful enough, but that was only the beginning of their irresolvable conflict. I believe it was their unwillingness to deal with this conflict in a healthy way that eventually led them into the much deeper pit of pain.

The process was as predictable as it was painful to watch. First they became withdrawn. Then they started missing the social gatherings and the weekly assemblies. Eventually they started shutting out their closest friends. Finally, Jennifer and John became sexually estranged and divorce became their last remaining option.

The night she told me about her plans to divorce him is etched in my brain forever. My family and I were in the chaotic midst of moving to another state and it was our last night in town together. We went out to a nice Italian restaurant and feasted on pasta, just like old times. Afterwards we went to their townhouse for a cup of coffee, dragging out the evening as far as we could. No one really wanted to say goodbye.

Jennifer abruptly asked if we could take a walk together. So we went outside and inhaled deeply the warm summer air. I thought she was going to ask me for advice about her relationship to John, especially the spiritual side of that relationship. I sensed their relationship was becoming strained, but not *that* strained. I even thought she wanted to pray together for John's soul.

I guess I never really saw it coming at all.

THE STORY

Like Jennifer, many women in biblical times had to deal with the problem of childlessness and the depression that accompanies it. As the story of Hannah unfolds in 1 Samuel, however, the narrator makes it clear to us that barrenness is just the beginning of Hannah's problems. Hannah's barrenness is really the springboard for three other problems: her rival Peninnah, her husband Elkanah, and her minister Eli. All fail her miserably. All bring her grief. All compound her pain. None seems to know how to help her.

Like Job with his three "friends," Hannah has to deal with *her* three "friends," and the result is one of the Bible's most memorable stories.

HANNAH AND PENINNAH

As a general rule, the ancients are not kind to barren women. In Israel, it is very difficult to be a barren wife, where so much of a woman's value is measured by the number and even the sex of the children she can bear her family. Imagine what it must have been like to have to share a house with a rival, fertile wife at the same time! Achingly childless, Hannah has to face the daily pain of watching someone else experience what she cannot. Peninnah basks in the maternal joy of not one, but several children. Peninnah gets to watch her children roughhouse with their father and learn their ABCs. Peninnah gets to feel the deep maternal love that only a mother can feel when her child is sick and cries out for help.

Not Hannah. For Hannah, life with Peninnah only makes an already painful situation even more unbearable.

As we've already seen, Elkanah's house looks a lot like Abraham's and Jacob's. Abraham's wife Sarah has to tolerate the "contempt" of her maid Hagar when she finds out about her pregnancy (Gen. 16:1-6). And Jacob's wife Leah has to live with the knowledge that she will never be Jacob's favorite. Each one of these marital relationships in Scripture harbors a potential for conflict and violence (see Gen. 29:31-35).

Historically, domestic relationships like these, while terribly foreign to us, were common in Hannah's day because they helped to provide social "safety valves" for the many small tribal peoples struggling to survive in the vastly underpopulated ancient Near East. Primarily for economic and sociological reasons, bearing children was simply more important than strict monogamy in ancient times. Yet polygamy always comes with a price. Much like the problems which plague "blended" families today, conflict between rival wives in the ancient Near East served up a vast array of thorny problems.[1] Several lawcodes deal expressly with these problems, and try to provide some sort of direction with regard to recurring domestic disputes over inheritance rights, levirate obligations, and other conflicts.[2]

Yet Peninnah's behavior, while explainable, is still reprehensible. It reminds me of the reception some missionary friends of mine once had to endure on their return to the States. Childless and

116

weary, they, like Hannah, felt badly about coming to church. Whenever they did someone would always ask, "When are you two kids going to quit fooling around and have a baby?" It was too much for them to bear.

Is anyone surprised to hear that they've never gone back to the mission field?

Let me put it another way. Doesn't the world have enough Peninnahs in it already?

HANNAH AND ELKANAH

To be sure, Elkanah is not an evil man, only a thick one.

"Hannah, stop crying. Hannah, eat. Hannah, isn't being married to me enough? Do you really need to be a mother, too? Am I not worth more to you than ten sons?" (1 Sam. 1:8).

How nice it would have been if Hannah had been given a warm, sensitive husband to help her deal with her pain and her rival's compounding of that pain. What she gets is Elkanah, the "Archie Bunker" of the Bible.[3] Blissfully ignorant of his wife's feelings, Elkanah does what many husbands do. He assumes that he ought to be the center of his wife's universe, so what's her problem? That's what wives are for, aren't they? To wait on their husbands hand and foot, right?

Perhaps, for the sake of argument, Hannah does need to hear what Elkanah has to say. OK. But does she need to hear it *now*? At the lowest point in her life? Would not other words be more helpful first? Doubtless somewhere along her spiritual journey she needs to confront her barrenness and the intense issues of identity and sexual frustration that it arouses. But Elkanah shows little awareness of where Hannah is on her spiritual journey. He doesn't know what to say or how to say it. He doesn't want to listen to her or help her carry her burden for a moment.

He doesn't realize that in matters of this kind "the wise of heart is called a man of discernment" (Prov. 16:21).

He may be a good man at heart, and he may genuinely love her. But Elkanah lacks spiritual discernment. At best, he could probably do well by saying nothing. At the very least, he could try to pick a more appropriate time to talk to his wife about their common problem.[4]

Dick and Diane O'Connor tell the story of a dinner party in the home of another couple. After the four of them finish dinner, they sit and chat for a while until the hour grows late. Then the O'Connors excuse themselves to leave, and the man of the house escorts them to the door. Sharing their final goodbyes, they start to go out the door when they suddenly realize that he fully intends to leave with them! It turns out he wants to catch the end of a hockey game at a local tavern with his buddies.

Thus the evening closes on a decidedly sour note for at least three of these people:

> We looked back to say good-night to his wife. She was standing in the doorway with a strange, sad smile on her face. Her husband didn't realize what he was putting her through. She must have seen our eyes. But here was her dilemma: she didn't want to end an otherwise pleasant evening with an ugly scene. So she was forced into humiliating silence. She became as spineless as the wet dishrag she would soon have to pick up.[5]

Well, let's put on our thinking caps, shall we? All together now. Can anyone identify this husband's problem? What shall we call it? I call it "Elkanah complex." Yes. This man has a classic case of "Elkanah-complex." And is this a rare disease? No, it's quite common, actually, as widespread as the common cold. The symptoms are easy to identify: (1) he fails to understand that marriage is a covenant relationship between two people, not a source of gratification for one; and (2) failing to understand this, he begins to take his wife more and more for granted.

"Elkanah" is more of a problem than a solution, more a burden than a burden-bearer in Hannah's life.

HANNAH AND ELI

Finally we come to Eli, Hannah's minister. By this point in the narrative perhaps we would like to think that *someone* in this situation will take the time to listen to this troubled woman. If neither Peninnah or Elkanah know what they're doing, *surely* Hannah's minister will take the time to understand her conflict and help her work through it. Ministers are trained to be sensitive, right?

Ministers always care, right?

Not Hannah's minister. Eli is too fixated on his own agenda to minister to anyone else. Little information is given us in the context, but from what we have Eli appears to have major problems of his own to deal with. His two sons, perhaps in emulation of their father, perhaps not, regularly embezzle food from the Lord's altar, and even seduce the Israelite women who bring it. Like several other fathers in the Bible, Eli has difficulty exercising a positive influence in his own home.[6] Practically speaking, this means that he not only is unable to minister to Hannah; he probably won't be of much help to anyone.

Whatever the reasons, the priesthood is eventually taken away from his family and given to another (1 Sam. 2:27-36).[7]

Eli is an interesting minor character. He may be a priest, but he certainly is not a minister of reconciliation. Just watch him at work. He takes Hannah to be drunk when in fact she's pouring out her soul to God in prayer. Then, instead of asking her about her problem, or showing her the tiniest inkling of human warmth, he jumps to a false conclusion and curtly rebukes her for a sin she has not even committed. When he finally does begin to realize the depth of her problem, he avoids personal involvement like the plague:

"Go in peace. May God grant your petition" (1 Sam. 1:17).

For all its religiosity, this response looks very much like another infamous maxim in Scripture:

"Go in peace. Be warmed and filled" (James 2:16).

We don't know much more than this, but whatever model for ministry Eli might be following here, it doesn't work.[8] Should God be merciful to Hannah and grant her a child (which he does), the narrator harbors little hope that Eli will have anything to do with the dispensing of God's divine grace. This potential channel is just too clogged up to be of much real use.

Eli is an example of how *not* to minister to someone in the throes of a conflict.[9]

In sum, Hannah's inner conflict is compounded and intensified by her external conflicts. Peninnah's fertility intensifies her barrenness, reminding her of her apparent worthlessness to her husband and herself. Elkanah, instead of empathizing with her pain, instead basks in his own self-centeredness, completely oblivious to his wife's needs. Eli, the minister who should have taken the time to listen and help, instead rebukes, condemns, and dismisses her for something over which she has no control.

CONFLICT RESOLUTION

Thus Hannah comes to the same point in her life to which Jennifer came. Yet why does one woman turn to God and the other to a divorce lawyer? What can explain the difference between such diametrically opposed responses to the same problem?

Let's be realistic. Hannah does not have to turn to God and pour out her soul in prayer. Nor does she have to promise her child to the Lord in perpetual service. She certainly does not have to tolerate the antics of Peninnah, the insensitiveness of Elkanah, or the indifference of Eli. She *can* decide, like Jennifer, to turn away from God, give up on God's people, and run away from her problems into a perpetual state of denial.

And to be sure, the church needs to develop a greater empathy for childless couples in our midst. According to one source I've read, approximately one out of every six couples in the United States suffers from childlessness. This is an astoundingly high statistic. Its source, John Van Regenmorter, thinks that the church is far too insensitive to its implications, and needs to change. Himself childless for many years, he begs us to be more careful with the Word on this subject,[10] more cautious with our advice to the childless, and more willing to listen to the pain suffered by childless couples.[11]

Yet no solution to Hannah's conflict can be deemed holistic if it ignores the factor of personal responsibility and personal faith. After all is said and done, Jennifer, like Hannah, needs to make a decision. She needs to work through her problem, not deny it. She needs to decide whether being a mother is more important than being a wife. She needs to decide whether being a mother is more important than being a Christian. She needs to decide whether being a Christian is more important than being "happy."

Only with God's help will she find the wisdom to decide what to do about the "Peninnahs" in her life. Only with God's help will she develop the compassion she needs to love John ("Elkanah") in spite of his almost comical callousness. Only with God's help will she develop the maturity she needs—and we all need—to look behind "Eli's" foibles and flaws and revere the God he so poorly represents anyway.

Only faith can make the barrenness more bearable.[12]

QUESTIONS FOR DISCUSSION

(1) Without naming names, do you know any "Peninnahs"? Describe what you think "makes her tick."
(2) Do you know any "Elkanahs"? Describe.
(3) Do you know any "Elis"? Describe.
(4) What enables Hannah to resolve her conflict?
(5) What can the church do to become more sensitive to the needs of childless couples today?
(6) Do you think John will ever become a Christian?

ENDNOTES

[1]Nicholas Zill and his colleagues have learned through careful research that children who live with their stepparents are at much greater risk today than children who live in single-parent environments. Zill's research is referenced in the important study of Barbara Dafoe Whitehead, "Dan Quayle Was Right," *The Atlantic Monthly* 271, 4 (April 1993) pp. 71-72.

[2]For further study, see Victor P. Hamilton's informative article on "Marriage in the Old Testament and the Ancient Near East" in *The Anchor Bible Dictionary*, vol. 4 (New York: Doubleday, 1992) pp. 559-569.

[3]A reference to the main character in the American television series *All In The Family*.

[4]Though barrenness is never portrayed as a "common problem" in Scripture.

[5]Dick and Diane O'Connor, *How To Make Your Man More Sensitive* (New York: E. P. Dutton and Co., 1975) pp. 4-5.

[6]For further study, see Paul A. Mickey and Ginny W. Ashmore, *Clergy Families: Is Normal Life Possible?* (Grand Rapids: Zondervan, 1991). I am indebted to Larry Snow for providing me with this reference.

[7]Paul Avis has a thorough, perceptive discussion of this point in his book *Authority, Leadership and Conflict in the Church* (Philadelphia: Trinity Press International, 1992) pp. 107-132.

[8]With regard to ministry models today, Bruce Shelley documents with concern the shift in American ministry models from "pastor-theologian" to "professional minister" to "enterprising healer." See his article "The Seminaries' Identity Crisis," in *Christianity Today* 37, 6 (May 17, 1993) pp. 42-44.

[9]For further study, see Rita-Lou Clarke, *Pastoral Care of Battered Women* (Louisville, KY: Westminster/John Knox, 1991).

[10]For example, to avoid preaching from traditional Mother's Day texts like Psalm 127:3 ("children are a heritage from the Lord") in a way that implies that childlessness is a curse from God.

[11]John Van Regenmorter, "Let's Stop Childless Abuse," *Christianity Today* 37, 2 (Feb 8, 1993) p. 15.

[12]For further study of this very sensitive issue, see Charles M. Sell's discussion in *Transitions Through Adult Life* (Grand Rapids: Zondervan, 1991) pp. 113-117.

DAVID'S INNER CONFLICT

(2 SAMUEL 11:1-12:23)

"Got a minute?"

"Sure, Tim, come on in."

The semester was drawing to a close and students had been jamming my office all day with typical last minute requests:

"My term paper's going to be late. That's OK, isn't it?"

"You don't mind if I skip the final exam, do you? I promised my fiancée I'd go home with her this weekend."

"I just heard that you count off for spelling. That's not true, is it?"

"What!? You expected me to write in paragraphs?"

Tim had popped in during the rush of all this scholarly activity, so I expected to hear something similar from him: he had just broken a finger, or worse, his typist had unexpectedly left town to visit Mom for a few weeks.

I soon learned differently.

Tim loves people. He loves God. He loves the Bible. He loves learning about the God revealed on its pages. Shy and reserved, he usually waits until the classroom has emptied before asking a question or voicing an opinion. Tim is one of those rare Christians who dares to *think*, really *think* about God. I respect him for his intellectual integrity as well as his strong, deep faith.

His "problem," as he put it, began early in life. At first, he didn't see anything wrong with it. No one told him it could be dangerous. By late adolescence, however, it was beginning to take over his mind and heart. Before long, it had him cornered—like a tough drill sergeant over a defenseless recruit.

Now it affected everything—the way he looked at his wife, his 13-year-old daughter, the secretary at the desk downstairs, the woman at the checkout counter, the deacon's wife two pews to the left.

He had hoped that the decision to enroll in seminary would solve it. It didn't. Seminary just made it worse. Seminary life only sensitized his conscience to ever higher levels of shame. He suspects that something is terribly wrong inside, but he doesn't know what to do about it. He prays constantly that he might learn how to "buffet" his body into submission. But he's discovering how difficult it is to rein in a body that's been allowed for years to have anything it wants.[1]

Whenever he sees a certain kind of film, whenever he reads a certain kind of magazine, whenever he drives past a certain kind of bookstore, it gnaws at his soul like a ravenous demon. He's falling deeper and deeper into its grasp. He feels like a man adrift at sea, paddling furiously away from a terrifying whirlpool of guilt and shame. Every time he tries to swim away, the thing just keeps sucking him back in.

Tim has lost control of what Michel Quoist calls simply "the body's hunger."[2]

Is his "problem" unusual? My own limited counseling experience tells me no. In fact, it's becoming more and more of a problem today, especially among men. We could list many reasons for this. Lack of parental teaching. Lack of role models. Lack of discipline.[3] But Tim's culture is to blame, too. In fact, one of Tim's most persistent dilemmas is the simple fact that he lives where he does—in a sex-satiated society bombarded daily by every imaginable kind of pornographic stimulus.[4]

No, Tim's problem is becoming more and more "usual" today, not unusual. It saturates the books we read, the films we see, and the music we hear.[5] It relentlessly corrupts our youth.[6] It corrodes our marriages, violates our sisters, and abuses our children. It crowds our hospitals, endangers our health care system, and paralyzes our political process.[7]

The Bible speaks of it often. It goads the inhabitants of Sodom into astonishing acts of violence (Gen. 19:5). It taunts Shechem into "humbling" Dinah (Gen. 34:2). It lunges at Joseph through a bored politician's wife (Gen. 39:7). It entices Israel's male population into a summer of "free love" on the plains of Moab (Num. 25:1-3). It humiliates Samson before his family and tribe (Judg. 16:17). It convinces Amnon that it's OK to rape his own half-sister (2 Sam. 13:14).

It tricks Herod Antipas into murdering a prophet he genuinely respects (Matt. 14:1-12). Failure to confront it openly practically paralyzes the Corinthian church (1 Cor. 5:1-5). From Romans to Revelation it sloshes through the streets of the Mediterranean world like an open sewer, infecting everything in its path with its deadly virus (see Rom. 1:18-32; Rev. 2:19-22; 17:1-18). Jesus of Nazareth warns his disciples repeatedly about its power (Matt. 5:27-30; 19:1-12).

THE STORY

For the typical Sunday School graduate, myself included, David is unquestionably the greatest of all Israelite kings. The obedient, faithful side of this saint has been pounded into our heads for as long as we can remember. David is the "sweet singer of Israel," the courageous young giant-killer, the "man after God's own heart" (1 Sam. 13:14; Acts 13:22).[8] All this is true.

So we might be forgiven for forgetting that he is still a human being. The temptation to read his life through rose-colored glasses is great. It's difficult for us to admit that he has a darker side. It's especially difficult for us to see that David has a "problem." But he does, and we need to find out why.

To put it bluntly, David has a problem with women. This is not a problem common to all men in the Old Testament, but it is a problem for David. Other Israelites know how to treat women. One has only to read the *Song of Songs* to see how men and women ought to treat one another.[9] Men can be tender and caring in Scripture, even in the supremely patriarchal world of the Old Testament. Contrary to popular belief, Old Testament males are not all brute beasts and sexist pigs.[10]

David, however, is not like the author of the *Song*. Take, for example, his relationship to Michal, Saul's daughter. Michal loves him, protects him, and endures for him the humiliation of having to live with another man. (See 1 Sam. 18:20; 19:11,14; 25:44.) Yet David never gives her a second thought until it's politically convenient for him to do so. Only when he realizes how useful she can be in securing his flank against the possibility of revenge from Saul's family does he decide to take her back into his harem (2 Sam. 3:14). The women in this harem eventually include Michal, Ahinoam, Abigail, Maacah, Haggith, Abital, Eglah and Bathsheba (2 Sam. 3:2-5).

That this relationship is motivated more by politics than romance becomes quite obvious in the scene where David leads the ark of the covenant into Jerusalem (2 Sam. 6:1-23). Caught up in the excitement of the occasion, David strips down to his shorts and dances wildly in front of Israel's most sacred icon. Michal, however, becomes utterly disgusted by this, and accuses him of staging a vulgar display for the benefit of Jerusalem's female population (2 Sam. 6:20).[11] Whether Michal should have said anything or not, we are still taken by surprise at the viciousness in his response to his wife. It shows us a side of this "man after God's own heart" that we would rather not see:

> I dance[12] before the Lord, who chose me instead of your father and all his house, to appoint me as prince over Israel. I am playing and dancing before the Lord. I can embarrass and humiliate you further in front of the ladies you've mentioned . . . . I'm admired among them (2 Sam. 6:21-22).[13]

Literally hundreds of parallels to David's behavior might be cited. One Sumerian king, for example, is bold enough to claim that even the goddess of love Inanna, should he decide to take her into *his* harem as wife, would never get away with telling *him* what to do.[14]

Thus we need to be careful not to lift this story out of its historical context. Regardless of what you or I might feel about David, the fact is that this king behaves very much like like any other Oriental monarch. Before we seek to apply this story to the contemporary world we must try to understand what it meant in David's world. The tendency to reduce faith solely to matters of individual morality and individual ethics is a peculiarly Western temptation, and should not be allowed to dictate interpretation.

So we need to be careful. A reading strategy more in tune with the story's historical context raises questions which need to be addressed thoroughly before we begin to pepper this text with *our* questions. *Our* questions, while pressing to us, may not be the most appropriate questions to ask of this ancient Israelite text, at least not at first.[15]

Some of the questions which arise from the text itself are these: What is it about David's affair with Bathsheba that *most* offends God? What is the nature of the link, if any, between adultery and murder? What is there about this incident that so angers Yahweh that he immediately responds by sending a prophet (Nathan) to confront the king directly for this particular sin?

ADULTERY

Adultery nauseates God. Adultery is an act of violence. As soon as a married person decides to give himself or herself to another person, the person's innocent spouse is unavoidably, brutally, and viciously violated. Words are quite inadequate to describe the intensity of God's feelings on this matter. Contrary to overwhelmingly popular opinion, families stricken by adultery and divorce do not bounce back very well from it. As Judith Wallerstein and others are systematically documenting through careful longitudinal study, families violated by adultery and divorce *always* suffer some degree of irreparable damage.[16]

Adultery is most contemptible, however, because of what it does to the Christian faith. At root, the Christian faith is a life based on *loyalty*. When we become Christians, we voluntarily enter into a covenant relationship with the same God who initiated covenants with our spiritual ancestors—men and women like Noah, Sarah, Abraham, Moses, Miriam.[17] Granted, the new covenant foretold by the prophets and ultimately fulfilled in Christ eliminates the need for physical ritual as a reminder of our covenant obligations. This ritual is now replaced by the all-sufficient sacrifice of Christ (Heb. 8:1-10:18). But in no way does Christ's sacrifice eliminate the obligations themselves. Christ rather *transforms* them to a more overtly spiritual plane in order to make them accessible to non-Jews.[18]

When you and I become Christians, we solemnly pledge our allegiance to a *covenant*. We voluntarily take on a degree of personal responsibility to be faithful to its provisions. Similarly, when you and I enter into a marriage covenant, we solemnly pledge to stay faithful to one person before the eyes of a covenant-making, covenant-keeping God.[19]

Consequently, when you or I willfully decide to violate these covenant obligations, we proclaim to the world that we no longer believe in the biblical God. Adultery is ultimately an act of disloyalty. Regardless of what yours or my "extenuating circumstances" might be, when we violate covenant we violate God, and boldly declare our allegiance to some other god made in our own image. Scripture is very clear about this. This is not a peripheral teaching. It lies at the very center of the Bible. Every prophet from Elijah to Jesus insists that someday each one of us will have to stand before the one true God and explain to him why we have chosen either to accept or reject his covenant love.[20]

Now, applying the ideal of *covenant* to the real world has always been a difficult thing to do. Medieval thinker Thomas Aquinas tried it and his attempt still makes a lot of sense. Aquinas argued that marriage was healthy for society for several reasons: (1) it takes human sexuality out of the bestial realm of violence and into the human realm of peaceful order; (2) it provides a way for women to be treated as full partners instead of sexual slaves; and (3) it points the way, through the faithfulness of each spouse to the marriage covenant, to the faithfulness of God in eternal covenant to his creation.

One does not have to look very far to see that all three of these principles are under attack today.[21]

Note also that when covenants are concluded in Scripture, a period of testing always follows. As soon as Yahweh and Israel enter into the Sinai covenant, a whole series of violations quickly follow. Moses states in his farewell address that one of the reasons Israel had to wander in the wilderness was so that Yahweh might test them, "to know what was in your heart, whether you would keep his commandments or not" (Deut. 8:2). The golden calf incident tested whether Israel wanted to worship Yahweh or some other god. The incident at Baal Peor tested them near the end of their wilderness sojourn. The incident with Achan tested Israel to see whether they were willing to give up their persistent covetousness.

(See Exod. 32:1-35; Num. 25:1-18; Josh. 7:1-26.)

Similarly, David's adultery with Bathsheba is the first major test of God's covenant with David (2 Sam. 7:4-17). When David fails this test and decides in spite of the covenant to seize another man's wife, David directly tests God.[22] David thinks he can interpret God's promise never to take away his "steadfast love" as an open license to do whatever he pleases (2 Sam. 7:15). God's response, however, is to summon Nathan the prophet. Technically speaking, Yahweh is not obligated to respond at all. Had David tried this at Sinai, he probably would have been put to death, along with the other offenders. (See Exod. 32:28.) Yet even as a father can hardly choose not to discipline a child he loves, God's love is such that he, too, gives David a chance to change.[23]

MURDER

Careful readers know that much more is said about Uriah in this story than Bathsheba. In my view, this is because the narrator wants us to dwell more fully on the *consequences* of covenant disloyalty than the disloyalty itself. Notice how the covenant loyalty of Uriah brilliantly highlights the covenant disloyalty of David. Uriah represents all that is good and holy about this covenant-keeping God. Uriah is a righteous foil to David's stubborn sinfulness.

After David impregnates Bathsheba, he tries to cover up his sin by arranging for Uriah to take military leave, something that normally involves spending time at home with one's wife. David hopes in this way that no one will be able to question later whether Uriah is the legitimate father of the child already growing in Bathsheba's womb.

Like Saul with Jonathan, however, David fails to reckon with Uriah's fervent *loyalty*. Heightening the irony, the narrator laboriously contrasts the loyalty of Uriah, a foreigner, with the disloyalty of David, the quintessential Hebrew.[24] David tries not once, but several times to convince Uriah to go home. And each time Uriah responds by reciting his loyalty to Yahweh.

The upshot of these contrasts is that Uriah is portrayed as the prototypical "righteous foreigner," utterly devoted to the God of Israel.[25] His is the fervor of the new convert, the brand-new brother still excited about his faith. Innocently responding to David's deceit, he unknowingly carries his own death warrant to Joab. The narrator wants us to linger a long time on this man's character because he wants to show us, by a series of pointed contrasts, just how despicable David's behavior is.

Further, Uriah has a specific reason for refusing to sleep with his wife. He's a holy warrior. In the ancient world, holy warriors always abstain from sexual contact during battle. Ahimelech makes this clear when he allows David's men to eat in Yahweh's sanctuary only after David assures him that they have "kept themselves from women" (1 Sam. 21:4). Martial celibacy is an important attribute of the holy warrior because normal familial relationships hold the danger of turning into precarious entanglements which enemies can use. Later Oriental despots even castrate their servants in order to protect themselves from their enemies.[26]

David knows this. His very attempt to convince Uriah otherwise shows how far he has drifted from the ideals of his youth. David used to be a holy warrior, too, back in the days when he kept covenant with Yahweh and lead Israel to greatness. Now he's a bored, complacent, ruthless old man who's interested only in saving his own skin, regardless of who gets in the way.

David Halberstam, in his bestselling book *The Powers That Be*, tells a revealing story about William Paley, the founder of CBS.[27] As Halberstam tells it, Paley could be charming and civilized, as familiar with the score of *Camelot* as the number of affiliate stations tied into his fledgling network. Meticulous and shrewd, Paley was one of the few media entrepreneurs who successfully negotiated the leap from radio to television.

Yet he could be ruthless. Once he and Ralph Colin, an attorney who served him loyally for forty years, had a dispute. Both men were serving on the board of the Metropolitan Museum of Art at the time when Paley rather peremptorily fired a trustee of the museum without consulting the board. Colin dared to ask him about it, and Paley responded by calling him into the office and firing him, too.

Asked later why he had been so cruel to one of his oldest friends, Paley was heard to have said, "Friends? We were never friends. Ralph was just my lawyer."

Such is the way David treats his "friends." If anything, he's even more ruthless. David descends to deceit, adultery and murder in order to hide himself from God and God's covenant—even if it means he has to squash a loyal, faithful servant like a bug. Hearing the news that Uriah has been "eliminated," his comment to Joab is just as icy as Paley's:

"Don't let it trouble you. The sword can devour anyone" (2 Sam. 11:25).

CONFLICT RESOLUTION

Here are the facts. Marital infidelity is at epidemic levels in the United States today. Alfred Kinsey shocked us in 1948 when he estimated that 50% of all American husbands had been at one time or another unfaithful to their wives.[28] Bernard Greene raised that number to 60%,[29] while Shere Hite, in an oft-quoted study of 7,239 men, reported in 1981 that a full 72% had at one time or another been unfaithful to their marriage vows.[30]

Frank Pittman offers an explanation for this that categorizes adulterers into four basic groups: the "accidental adulterer," the "philandering adulterer," the "romantic adulterer," and the "maritally ambivalent adulterer." The first lives in a state of guilt and anxiety, the second in anger, the third in romantic longing, and the fourth in a complex combination of all three emotions.[31]

Everyone agrees that there's a problem. The differences come in deciding what to do about it. Carol Botwin, for example, has personally experienced the pain of infidelity, including the emotional and sexual abandonment that comes with it. A well-known advice columnist, her book, *Men Who Can't Be Faithful*, is carefully stocked with helpful, practical advice on how to find out whether an unfaithful spouse is willing to change. She talks about how to identify and remove hidden agendas, how to agree to be honest, how to use language that defuses, how to be specific about goals, how to listen, and how to address differing sexual needs.

But Botwin's approach assumes (1) that men *cannot*, not simply *will not*, but *cannot* be faithful, and (2) that relationships can always be restored back to health simply by identifying the problem areas and talking them through.[32]

Peggy Vaughan is another survivor of marital betrayal. When

she writes, her primary concern is for the "innocent" spouse who tends to take personal blame for the break-up of the marriage. For people who think their marriage falls apart simply because they aren't sexy enough, smart enough, or just plain good enough, Vaughan seeks to lay primary blame for the problem at the feet of what she calls the "monogamy myth."

> The monogamy myth is the belief that monogamy is the norm in our society and that it is supported by society as a whole. The effect of believing that most marriages are monogamous is that if an affair happens, it's seen strictly as a personal failure of the people involved. This leads to personal blame, personal shame, wounded pride, and almost universal feelings of devastation.[33]

Vaughan's approach assumes (1) that the primary responsibility for adultery is societal, not personal, and (2) that societal norms are the only real norms that matter.

In sharp contrast to both these approaches, Scripture teaches that *repentance + confession* is the only acceptable solution to the sin of adultery. Both of the solutions just cited fundamentally fail to recognize this as a workable solution because both are grounded in a secularist worldview. Neither Botwin nor Vaughan have room in their minds for a God who created the universe and sustains it by the word of his power, much less a God who initiates, maintains, repairs, and holds people accountable to a holy covenant.

For Christians, however, any attempt at conflict resolution which ignores the reality of God and the reality of God's covenant-keeping character is insufficient, naive, idolatrous and heretical.

Nathan confronts David in his famous "Thou art the man" speech in order to warn David that his soul is in danger (2 Sam. 12:1-12). David has broken covenant with Yahweh. Thus, David's fear of reprisal and love for the Lord meld together in an instantaneous decision to change his behavior. In 2 Samuel 12:13, he responds to Nathan's indictment with the all-important confession, "I have sinned."

Note it carefully. *Repentance* . . . and *confession*.

Fortunately, Scripture preserves a more extended response in the 51st Psalm. A close reading of this psalm is a study in contrast between David's response to adultery and those recommended by

Carol Botwin and Peggy Vaughan.

First, David deeply *laments* the sin he has committed. Instead of blaming society, blaming Bathsheba, or blaming God, he blames himself for what he has done. Wonder of wonders, he dares to take personal responsibility for his behavior. He recognizes immediately that to wallow in self-pity, to whine to God about his "rights" as a "victim" does absolutely nothing to repair covenant. Facing his sin squarely is the only way David can find the perspective he needs to raise his eyes high enough to discover the source of his conflict:

"Against you, and you only have I sinned, and done that which is evil in your sight" (Ps. 51:4).

To argue, with Peggy Vaughan, that the party most hurt by an adulterous affair is the "innocent" spouse is to offer a narcissistic and adolescent response to one of the most debilitating problems of our time. Fundamentally, it is to blind oneself to the feelings of a living God.[34] All Christians know that the Father is heartbroken when one of his children breaks covenant with him. We have to look no farther than the Cross to see this pain. The world will never understand this. It takes a great deal of faith to recognize this, particularly when one's emotional life is battered and bludgeoned by a marital crisis.

Second, after David laments the brokenness of his covenant with God, he dares to ask him for another chance at relationship:

"Create in me a clean heart, O God . . . .

Cast me not from your presence . . . .

Restore to me the joy of your salvation . . ." (Ps. 51:10-12).

Unlike Carol Botwin, David refuses to accept the view that men *cannot* be faithful. To believe this is to believe that all human behavior is predetermined, that human beings are mechanically predestined to live in pain, that none of us has the ability to live our lives without the free will to change. David rejects this worldview. David knows he has sinned, but he doesn't wallow in it. He dares to believe, in the midst of his pain, in the possibility of spiritual change. He refuses to allow sin to turn him into a skeptic.

Finally, David promises to keep covenant in the future:

Then I will teach transgressors your ways and sinners will return to you. Deliver me from bloodguilt, O God of my salvation, and my tongue will sing aloud of your deliverance (Ps. 51:13-14).

With Paul, David commits to the view that "worldly sorrow" is prevalent, but powerless. Only "godly sorrow" can effect real change in the stubborn human heart, however broken or confused it might be.[35] "Talking it out," though a necessary first step toward *identifying* the parameters of a conflict, never really *resolves* conflict. Even some secular psychologists are coming to realize this.[36] Conflict *identification* does not equal conflict *resolution*. Our problem remains the stubborn sinfulness of our hearts. Only God can change us. We cannot change ourselves. To ignore this truth is to remain tragically naive to the overwhelming power of sin as well as the redemptive power of the Word of God.[37]

Reconciliation becomes an option only when adulterers, like all other sinners, decide to take personal responsibility and repair the covenant they have broken. This is why this story has been preserved in Scripture, to show us, when we fall, how to find our way out of sin's sticky web of lies and deceit and heartache and violence.

Like David, we all need to *repent* and *confess* when we break covenant with God. The first step addresses God. The second addresses God's people. The first focuses on repairing a damaged vertical relationship. The second focuses on repairing a damaged horizontal relationship.

Both have to be repaired if reconciliation is to become possible for "an evil and adulterous generation" (Matt. 12:39).

QUESTIONS FOR DISCUSSION

(1) In your opinion, how common is Tim's problem?
(2) Evaluate the responses of Carol Botwin and Peggy Vaughan to the problem of adultery.
(3) What really lies at the root of Tim's problem?
(4) What does the Church need to do to respond better to the problem of marital infidelity?
(5) Why is adultery so threatening to the Church?
(6) Evaluate Frank Pittman's four categories of adultery.
(7) Why are repentance *and* confession both essential to a biblical theology of reconciliation?

ENDNOTES

[1]See 1 Corinthians 9:27. Steve Rabey claims that "increasing numbers of people . . . enter the pastorate as a way of healing their own hurts," only to be disillusioned when this "solution" doesn't work; "Where the Hurting Pastors Go," *Christianity Today* 36 (Nov 23, 1992) p. 15.

[2]Michel Quoist, *With Open Heart* (translated by Colette Copeland; New York: Crossroad, 1983) p. 7.

[3]See Richard J. Foster, *Celebration of Discipline*, 2nd ed. (San Francisco: Harper, 1988) pp. 110-125.

[4]"The War Within: An Anatomy of Lust," *Leadership* 3, 4 (1982) pp. 41-42.

[5]See Michael Medved, *Hollywood vs. America: Popular Culture and the War on Traditional Values* (New York: Harper Collins/Zondervan, 1992).

[6]A 16-year-old pregnant high school dropout writes, "I know that things could have been different if I had had someone to talk to me about sex and its consequences or someone (like a mother) to teach me morals." *The Arizona Republic* (February 2, 1993) p. A9.

[7]David Neff claims that a sexually transmitted disease is now caught by an American teenager every 13 seconds in the United States. On average, one out of every 500 college students carries the HIV virus; "Will Your Child Get AIDS?" *Christianity Today* 33 (Sept 22, 1989) p. 11. Marcella Bakur Weiner and Bernard D. Starr argue that AIDS is still more prevalent among homosexuals than heterosexuals in *Stalemates: The Truth About Extra-Marital Affairs* (Far Hills, NJ: New Horizon Press, 1989) p. 139.

[8]Lynn Anderson emphasizes this side of David in his book *Finding the Heart to Go On* (San Bernardino, CA: Here's Life Publishers, 1991).

[9]See Joseph C. Dillow, *Solomon on Sex: The Biblical Guide to Married Love* (Nashville: Thomas Nelson, 1977).

[10]Carol Botwin believes that men, as a species, are brute beasts patently unable to control themselves; *Men Who Can't Be Faithful* (New York: Warner Books, 1988). How different is the portrayal in the *Song of Songs*. Eugene Peterson reminds us that the ancients were not at all embarrassed by genuine sexual intimacy. Unlike most secularists, however, they believed that "human love took its color from divine love"; *Five Smooth Stones for Pastoral Work* (Atlanta: John Knox, 1980) p. 40.

[11]Note how the Chronicler portrays a more fully-clothed David in 1 Chronicles 15:27.

[12]In this translation I am reading with the Septuagint, an early Greek translation of the Hebrew text.

[13]The passage concludes in verse 23 with the words, "and Michal the daughter of Saul had no child to the day of her death."

[14]See James Pritchard, ed., *Ancient Near Eastern Texts Relating to the Old Testament* (Princeton: University Press, 1969) p. 586.

[15]See Darrell Jodock, *The Church's Bible* (Minneapolis: Augsburg Fortress, 1989) pp. 18-19.

[16]See the important work of Judith Wallerstein and Sandra Blakeslee, *Second Chances: Men, Women and Children a Decade After Divorce* (New York: Ticknor and Fields, 1989) pp. 3-20. Annette Lawson offers a thorough sociological analysis in *Adultery* (New York: Basic Books, 1988).

[17]William J. Dumbrell, *Covenant and Creation: A Theology of Old Testament Covenants* (Nashville: Thomas Nelson, 1984) pp. 11-163.

[18]*Ibid.*, pp. 164-206.

[19]Assuming we decide to renounce our celibacy, a lifestyle which, if entered into voluntarily, has its own spiritual benefits. For further study, see M. S. Moore, "Marriage: Chance or Choice?" *Firm Foundation* 98 (1981) pp. 279, 295.

[20]See M. S. Moore, "Yahweh's Day," *Restoration Quarterly* 29 (1987) 193-208.

[21]Aquinas is cited and commented on in Walter Kaspar, *Theology of Christian Marriage* (New York: Crossroad, 1989) p. 8.

[22]See Deuteronomy 6:16, cited by Jesus to the devil in Matthew 4:7.

[23]Tim LaHaye discusses several other factors which contribute to adulterous affairs: the power of sexual attraction, the power of seductive women, the power of emotional bonding, pride, resistance to accountability, anger, the press for success, the drive to fulfill goals, workaholism, uncontrolled lust, addiction to pornography, and homosexuality; *If Ministers Fall, Can They Be Restored?* (Grand Rapids: Zondervan, 1990) pp. 35-61.

[24]Jesus uses this same technique in his first recorded sermon, contrasting the righteous behavior of two foreigners, Naaman the Syrian and the widow of Zarephath, with the unrighteous behavior of his Nazarene audience (Luke 4:25-27).

[25]Like Barzillai the Gileadite in 2 Samuel 19:31, or Tamar the Canaanite in Genesis 38:26, or Naaman the Syrian in 2 Kings 5:14.

[26]The Greek historian Xenophon describes this in his history of Cyrus' Asia Minor wars, called *Cyropaedia* (book 7, chapter 5, lines 58-61).

[27]New York: Alfred A. Knopf, 1979, pp. 29-31.

[28]Alfred C. Kinsey, Wardell B. Pomeroy, Clyde E. Martin and Paul H. Gebhard, *Sexual Behavior in the Human Male* (Philadelphia: W. B. Saunders, 1948).

[29]Bernard Greene, Ronald L. Lee and Noel Lustig, "Conscious and Unconscious Factors in Marital Infidelity," *Medical Aspects of Human Sexuality* (Sept 1974) 87-111.

[30]Shere Hite, *The Hite Report on Male Sexuality* (New York: Alfred A. Knopf, 1981).

[31]Frank Pittman, *Private Lies: Infidelity and the Betrayal of Intimacy* (New York: W. W. Norton, 1989) pp. 133-134.

[32]Carol Botwin, *Men Who Can't Be Faithful*, pp. 205-250.

[33]Peggy Vaughan, *The Monogamy Myth* (New York: Newmarket Press, 1989) p. 6.

[34]See Terence Fretheim, *The Suffering of God: An Old Testament Perspective* (Philadelphia: Fortress, 1984).

[35]"Godly sorrow produces a repentance that leads to healing and brings no regret, but worldly sorrow produces death" (2 Corinthians 7:10).

[36]For further study, see Robert C. Roberts, *Taking the Word to Heart: Self and Other in an Age of Therapies* (Grand Rapids: Eerdmans, 1993) pp. 15-150.

[37]See Donald G. Bloesch, "Total Depravity," in *Essentials of Evangelical Theology*, vol. 1 (New York: Harper and Row, 1978) pp. 88-119. For further study, see M. S. Moore, "Are Our Wounds Incurable? (Micah 1:9)" in Don Shackleford, ed., *Today Hear His Voice: The Minor Prophets Speak* (Harding University's 70th Annual Bible Lectureship; Searcy, AR: Harding University, 1993) pp. 313-324.

SAUL'S LEADERSHIP STYLE

(1 SAMUEL 13:1-20:42)

Lloyd rarely becomes angry.

Not visibly, anyway. He's too calm and even-handed, even when tempers around him flare and discussions grow heated.

One of Lloyd's gifts is the ability to weigh evidence and make difficult decisions. A leader in the church for years, he has often had to face unjustified, petty, even harsh criticism.

Yet even his critics cannot dislike him. Lloyd is not a vengeful man. Everyone who knows him knows that he cares deeply about the church and its mission to broken, hurting people. Everyone appreciates his gentle, temperate spirit.

Well, not everyone.

A few years ago there was a controversy in our church over how to share the Good News with others. Two parties arose in dispute over this question. One group attacked the other for what they felt was an abysmal lack of zeal. Unless we convert at least a hundred or more people a year, they argued, it is ridiculous for us to go on calling ourselves "Christians." We have to be involved in evangelistic activity every night of the week. We have to assign older "prayer partners" to newer believers in order to keep them faithful.

Others took offense at this position, arguing that it was much too rigid, resenting what they felt was the obvious: that numerical quotas are fine as goals, but not as laws; that "prayer partnering" is a good idea, but not a necessary statute; that Christian evangelism is much more than mere religious proselytism.

The labels flew fast and furious. One group branded the other as "passive" and "uncommitted." The other struck back with epithets like "zealot" and "legalist." Everyone involved in the dispute lamented the appalling lack of spiritual zeal draining the church of its life-blood. Not everyone was prepared, however, to sacrifice their blood-bought freedom in Christ to reclaim it.

People on both sides began turning to Lloyd for leadership, and he valiantly tried to provide it. Patiently pointing out, by personal as well as Scriptural example, that the primary mission of the Church is to call non-believers back to Christ, he scored a big hit with the "zealots." But when he also argued for the God-given freedom to decide how best to do it, he never got to first base.

Matters soon came to a head. The only time I ever saw Lloyd angry was the day he received a registered letter from the "zealot" party warning him to "repent" of his "sins," and threatening dire consequences if he did not.

I can still see the veins sticking out on his neck.

This all happened years ago, but the memory of that McCarthy-esque episode still causes a twinge of pain.[1] Running into Lloyd a few years later, I asked him whether he would approach the problem the same way today. Characteristically, he replied that he wished he had been more understanding, more patient, more compassionate with everyone involved.

Then he shrugged his shoulders, looked me straight in the eye and said,

"But conflict is sometimes inevitable, right?"

His statement caught me off guard. *Inevitable*? Is conflict sometimes inevitable? Even among Christians?

Whether we choose to admit it or not, the truth is that good Christian people don't always see eye to eye. Christians can and do argue over all sorts of things, from the profound to the petty. We argue over how to do evangelism, over how to raise children, over how to ascertain the beginning of life, over how to worship God, over how to train ministers, over how to interpret the Bible, over how to help the poor, over how to choose leaders, over how to handle money, over how to pay the preacher, over how to carpet our church buildings, over how to do this, over how to do that.

The list is endless. Whenever we can argue, we do argue. We're experts at it. Although Scripture has not spoken in absolute legal detail on a single one of the issues just listed, many twist themselves into pretzels trying to figure out God's will from what he has *not* said rather than what he *has*. Usually this involves twisting and bending Scripture to fit within some sort of Pharisaic, Aristotelian, or Baconian system of logic.[2]

But does conflict always have to lead to division? James urges us to "count it all joy" when our lives are tested by conflict (see James 1:2-4). Jesus prayed, however, in John 17:11, that his disciples might never experience division. How can these opposing statements be reconciled?

The truth is that conflict can be a healthy stimulus toward reigniting old, tired Christians and old, tired churches. This is what the "zealots" among us want to see. To some extent this is also what James has in mind. Conflict deteriorates into division, however, whenever we ignorantly or willfully seek to resolve it apart from the basic values which make us who we are, the values which distinguish us from the rest of the world, the values which make us truly Christian.

Before his own moment of supreme conflict, Jesus prayed fervently that his disciples might come to understand this, and surrender before the supreme Christian value, *love*. Paul builds on this in his powerful warning to the church in Galatia. Alongside the love that Jesus incarnated, he adds joy, peace, patience, kindness, goodness, faithfulness, gentleness, and self-control (Gal. 5:22-23). For Christians, these are the preeminent values upon which we rely to resolve our conflicts. To abandon them is to abandon Christ.[3]

THE STORY

Jonathan, son of Saul and crown prince of Israel, rarely becomes angry. He is much too temperate in disposition and character. His father, however, is another matter. Saul, the first king of Israel, is a fearful, troubled man, haunted by insecurity and imprisoned by rage. The story of his relationship to Jonathan is a strange one. On the surface, it looks much like the on-again-off-again relationship between David and Absalom. Underneath the surface, however, there are major differences. David is a passive, detached father, while Saul, if anything, is too involved. And Absalom is an angry, conniving adolescent who fights to preserve his rights at any cost—the exact opposite of Jonathan.

The history of their relationship has its own distinctive character.

In 1 Samuel 13, Saul imperiously takes credit for Jonathan's defeat of the Philistines at Geba, then tries to steal the glory for it in a "victory" ceremony at Gilgal. In chapter 14, Saul begins turning the tide against the Philistines, then unexplainably cripples his own army by refusing them food. In chapter 15, he claims to have devoted the spoils of a raid against the Amalekites wholly to God while sheep are "bleating" and cattle are "lowing" all around him. Confronted by Samuel, he then tries to shift responsibility for his sin onto the backs of his subjects.[4]

In chapter 16, the stress of the monarchy starts getting to Saul. His subordinates realize this and hire David to play the lyre and soothe his troubled mind. In chapter 17, he tries to convince David not to fight Goliath. Fortunately, he fails to dissuade him. In chapter 18, his smoldering insecurity over David breaks out into open flame. He inaugurates a series of political ploys to have David neutralized, manipulating his daughters like chattel in the process. In chapter 19, he suffers something of a mental breakdown, and hurls a spear at David in a fit of rage.

Finally, in chapter 20, Saul bitterly attacks his own son in a public tirade. Frustrated with Jonathan for befriending his rival, Saul finally falls over the edge of sanity altogether into the murky depths of manic depression. Like Captain Ahab in *Moby Dick*, Saul seems to have evolved into a man bent on destroying himself and everyone else around him in a mad quest to satisfy his own, insatiable needs.[5]

This story may not be as well known as others in Scripture, but several factors commend its preservation. It may be in our Bibles to warn later generations about the dangers of the monarchy, and the hierarchical principles by which it operates.[6] It may be in our Bibles to remind us that Yahweh's wrath is a mysterious power from which no human being, not even a king, can hide or escape.[7]

At root, however, the story of Saul seems to be a story about *leadership style*. Saul is a leader who doesn't lead very well, either because he doesn't know how, or because he refuses to learn how.

From an historical point of view, the problem of the monarchy was a matter never fully resolved in Israel. Like other ancient Near Eastern societies in transition, ancient Israel had great difficulty changing over from a tribal confederacy to a centralized monarchy.

Most Israelites eventually came to accept the monarchy as normative, but some never did. Saul son of Kish had the difficult task, some might say the supreme misfortune, of being the first leader entrusted to make the new system work.[8]

His story, therefore, is the story of Israel's struggle to decide a very basic question: What kind of leadership style do we want? What kind of leadership style is both faithful *and* relevant?

EARLY DOUBTS

1 Samuel 14 opens with an indecisive leader hopelessly paralyzed before a powerful enemy. Impatient over his father's indecision with regard to the Philistines, Jonathan decides to take matters into his own hands. He bravely assaults a garrison of the Philistines in a daring raid. The fact that he doesn't tell his father about it is carefully and purposefully noted in the text. (See 1 Sam 14:1.) The reason for this soon becomes clear. Jonathan and his colleagues harbor grave doubts about the competence of Saul's leadership abilities.

Following Jonathan's lead, Saul then involves himself in the battle which ensues. He seeks Yahweh's favor by consulting lots, the Urim ("No") and the Thummim ("Yes") lots stored in the ark of the covenant. This is a common preparation for war in the ancient Near East. Leaders rarely go into battle without first consulting the divine world for guidance.[9] Before the priest can pull a "yes" or a "no" out of the ark, however, Saul launches himself into the fray without fully ascertaining whether Yahweh approves, impetuously telling the priest, "Withdraw your hand" (1 Sam. 14:19).

This decision alienates the religious community.

After the battle gets under way, Saul tries another religious tactic. He invokes a curse on any man who refuses to fast. Doubtless he invokes this decree for pious reasons, but regardless of his motives, the result is the same. His army begins to lose its physical strength and cannot perform to its potential. Even the narrator notes that Saul's ill-planned fasting decree does little more than "oppress" Israel (1 Sam. 14:24). The word he uses for "oppress" is the same word used in Exodus to describe the Egyptian taskmasters who "oppressed" Israel centuries before (Exod. 5:16).

Thus Saul's first command offends the priesthood, while his second command offends the army.

His army, meanwhile, becomes hungry enough to bolt for the livestock and start eating it raw. The eating of blood is clearly forbidden in the law of Moses, so Saul is appropriately horrified.[10] Yet the thought never enters his mind that he might be at least partially responsible for causing their behavior. Instead of admitting responsibility, he retreats to a well-worn pattern. He starts looking for a scapegoat. He tries to search out, through the appropriate divinatory channels, who or what might be "troubling" Israel. The irony, of course, is that Saul himself is "the troubler."[11]

Meanwhile, Jonathan remains cool. Whatever he might be thinking internally, he is careful to say publicly only what others are thinking:

"My father is troubling the land" (1 Sam. 14:29).[12]

What turns out to be Saul's last chance to prove himself comes when Yahweh gives him another mission and commands him to rid Israel of the Amalekites. (See 1 Sam. 15:1-23.) But Saul blows this last chance. He violates Yahweh's decree and chooses the best of the spoil for himself. He violates the most important rule of "holy war," the requirement that *all* of the spoil be devoted to Yahweh. To us, this may look like a cruel custom, but in actuality it helps to check the spread of violence because it removes the economic incentive for waging war.

This is the last straw for Yahweh. "Repenting" of his decision to make Saul king, Yahweh instructs Samuel to find Israel another one, and Samuel begins the search which eventually culminates in the secret anointing of David.

THE POWER STRUGGLE

It is when David enters the picture, first as Saul's "therapist," then as his "savior," that Israel begins to discover in this lowly shepherd boy the leadership qualities so obviously lacking in Saul (1 Sam. 16:23; 17:50-54). David is courageous, yet not reckless. David is devout, yet not hypocritical. David is secure, yet not smug. David seems to live by faith, not fear.

At first, Saul is as excited as everyone else when Goliath's head is removed from his torso and the Philistines run for their lives. Yet how quickly his excitement turns to alarm. Deeply insecure, he knows he has alienated his priesthood, his army, and his family. He begins to suspect that something is radically wrong inside. Yet the way he chooses to resolve his conflict only makes a bad situation worse.

First, he tries to neutralize David by assigning him a field command over 1,000 men. As David does with Uriah later, Saul hopes in this way that his rival will be killed in battle, and his "problem" solved (2 Sam. 11:15).

When this doesn't work, he goes to "plan B." He plots to counter David's growing power by absorbing him directly into his family. As Laban does with Leah and Rachel in Genesis 29:15-30, Saul uses his daughters Merab and Michal to dangle the security of family and clan before David like carrots before a horse.

This doesn't work, either, so he goes to "plan C." Raising the ante, Saul demands that David kill 100 Philistines in order to win Michal's hand, hoping again that David will be killed in the process. But David's response is shrewd. He knows he has been foiled twice by this lying king, so he makes doubly sure this time that nothing will go wrong. He dramatically throws down not just 100, but 200 Philistine foreskins, outwitting his father-in-law and securing Michal's hand.

With each attempt, David grows in power while Saul sinks into deeper frustration. "Saul has killed his thousands, but David his ten-thousands" becomes the new national anthem (1 Sam. 18:7). He feels the kingdom slipping away from him, so he panics. He tries one last time to neutralize his rival. He tries something so vicious, so cruel, it makes all his previous attempts pale into insignificance. In 1 Samuel 19:1, he approaches Jonathan with a request ranking as one of the darkest moments in Jonathan's life.

He asks Jonathan to kill his best friend.

Cynical and jaded, Saul thinks he can appeal to Jonathan's darker side, the hidden desire in all of us for power and prestige. But Jonathan rarely becomes angry. He refuses to play Saul's political game. We get the impression, in fact, that Jonathan is tired of covering for his father, tired of bailing him out, tired of explaining away his incompetence.

In a speech much like Abigail's later, Jonathan eloquently pleads before the king for David's life, reminding his father of David's loyalty and bravery, as well as his own responsibility to treat him with justice (1 Sam. 19:4-5).

For a moment, it seems to work. Jonathan's words break through Saul's elaborate personal defenses. The king calms down and backs off.

But only for a moment.

TOTAL BREAKDOWN

Scriptural stories about tragic heroes often climax in a "point of no return." This is the point where, to use the language used above, conflict inevitably deteriorates into division. Biblical narrators use tragedy because tragedy is such a powerful literary vehicle for conveying desperate human need as well as the assurance of divine salvation. In the story of Joseph, it comes when Jacob's sons decide to sell their brother into slavery (Gen. 37:27). In the story of Uriah, it comes when David sends a note to Joab (2 Sam. 11:14). In the story of Jesus, it comes when Judas Iscariot kisses his master on the cheek (Matt. 26:15).

In the story narrated above, it comes when Lloyd receives a registered letter in the mail—that awful, crushing moment when all his hopes for reconciliation are suddenly dashed to pieces.

In the story of Saul, it comes when Saul publicly accuses his son of treason. What a powerful scene! This is the kind of scene an actor would give his right arm to play. The point of no return. The moment of truth. Jonathan has tried and failed to mediate the conflict between Saul and David. He has appealed to Saul on David's behalf. He has appealed to David on Saul's behalf. (See 1 Sam. 19:4-5; 20:2.) But none of his efforts can stay the inevitable. This becomes crystal clear when his father attacks him in the following tirade:

> You son of a perverse, rebellious woman! I know you have chosen the son of Jesse to your own shame, and the shame of your mother's nakedness! Your kingdom shall never be established. Not as long as the son of Jesse lives upon the earth! (1 Sam. 20:30-31, slightly paraphased).

The point of no return. The last straw. The point where conflict inevitably becomes division. This speech is a turning point in the narrative because it changes things forever between Saul and Jonathan. Stung by his father's words, Jonathan stands up from the banquet table, takes one last look at the princely life he knows he's leaving forever, and abandons his father to the mercies of God.

There's just nothing else he can do.

CONFLICT RESOLUTION

Leadership, even in its less stressful moments, is a "foul-weather job."[13] Human beings will always be sinful. Conflict will always be inevitable and conflict resolution will always be difficult. Competent leaders know this so they spend a great deal of time and energy trying to engage those with whom they disagree, not avoid them. They learn how to argue on principles, not personalities. They learn how to develop clear, realistic expectations about the parties and positions which they're constantly being asked to mediate.[14]

But how? How important it is that those who take up the mantle of leadership learn how to resolve conflict by faithful, courageous example instead of crass manipulation or outright deceit.[15] I believe that the issue in this text—and the issue of our day—is whether or how much a biblical ethic will be allowed to determine our leadership style.[16] Management specialists can be both a help and a hindrance here because some of them argue that seduction, redirection, and repudiation are acceptable leadership styles.[17]

Scripture, however, directly challenges this kind of "ends-justify-the-means" ethic. The story of Saul stands as a veritable indictment against it. The whole point of the story seems to be that Saul fails to lead because he chooses not to lead. If this is the point, then the application to us as ministers of reconciliation seems clear. Regardless of what we see all around us, regardless of what the specialists say, regardless of what we feel is right or wrong, *there simply is no place for a Saul-like leadership style in the churches, families, and businesses where we serve.* When we open the door to deceit, seduction, or manipulation in any form for any reason, we choose to engage in a leadership style which offends God. Max De

Pree puts it this way:

"Leaders don't inflict pain; they bear pain."[18]

Most importantly, leaders are entrusted with the task of conceiving, articulating, and implementing a vision for the future. Robert Dale, a specialist in helping churches learn how to do this, suggests several questions that we might ask ourselves in order to spark this envisioning process.

> What kind of Christians do I dream of? What kind of Church must I develop to grow my dream Christians? What kind of leadership team of volunteer and paid staff must I develop to grow my dream Christians? What kind of minister must I become to realize this dream?[19]

Jonathan's father makes half-hearted stabs at each one of these goals, but never really seems to take them seriously. That's why he fails. Saul lacks all three of these characteristics: *realistic expectations*, *high spiritual ethics*, and *vision*. Thus his leadership style perverts, reverts, and subverts itself into something terribly destructive and toxic. One of the major reasons why this story is preserved in Scripture is to show us that all three of these ingredients must remain firmly in view if we expect to retain a measure of competent, compassionate, Christian leadership today.

QUESTIONS FOR DISCUSSION

(1) How does Saul "use" religion?

(2) Contrast David's and Saul's leadership styles.

(3) What role does Jonathan play in this story?

(4) Do you know any "Sauls"? Describe.

(5) How would you have handled Jonathan's situation?

(6) Is conflict always bad? Why or why not?

(7) What is the difference between *conflict* and *division*?

ENDNOTES

[1]This is a reference to Senator Joseph McCarthy, the Wisconsin senator who was notorious in the 1950s for his Communist witch-hunts.

[2]See C. Leonard Allen, *The Cruciform Church: Becoming a Cross-Shaped People in a Secular World*, 2nd ed. (Abilene: ACU Press, 1990) pp. 19-79.

[3]Victor Paul Furnish says more about this in *Theology and Ethics in Paul* (Nashville: Abingdon, 1968). Charles B. Cousar elaborates further in A *Theology of the Cross: The Death of Jesus in the Pauline Letters* (Minneapolis: Fortress, 1990) pp. 135-175.

[4]Devoting an enemy totally to God, including women, children, and livestock, is characteristic of all "holy" wars. See Gerhard von Rad, *Holy War in Ancient Israel* (Grand Rapids: Eerdmans, 1991; first published in 1951).

[5]A reference to Herman Melville's classic novel, whose main character is very much modeled after Israel's first king.

[6]See 1 Samuel 8:10-18. Laurence J. Peter has written a classic analysis of the problems inherent to hierarchies in his books *The Peter Principle* (New York: Bantam, 1970), and *Why Things Go Wrong, or, The Peter Principle Revisited* (New York: Morrow, 1985).

[7]See David M. Gunn, *The Fate of King Saul* (Sheffield: Journal for the Study of the Old Testament Press, 1980).

[8]See Baruch Halpern, *The Constitution of the Monarchy in Israel* (Chico, CA: Scholars Press, 1981).

[9]See Herbert B. Huffmon, "Priestly Divination in Israel," in C. L. Meyers and M. O'Connor, eds., *The Word of the Lord Shall Go Forth: Essays Presented to David Noel Freedman* (Winona Lake, IN: Eisenbrauns, 1983) pp. 355-359.

[10]See Leviticus 19:26. The eating of blood is forbidden because of its association with witchcraft.

[11]In Joshua 7:1-26, Joshua uses a similar ritual to find another "troubler" of Israel. This is the story of Achan, who is called Achar ("the troubler") in 1 Chronicles 2:7.

[12]Literally, "My father is another 'Achar'."

[13]Peter Drucker, *Managing the Non-Profit Organization* (New York: HarperCollins, 1990) pp. 9-27.

[14]See Mark Juergensmeyer, *Fighting With Gandhi: A Step-By-Step*

Strategy for Resolving Everyday Conflicts (San Francisco: Harper and Row, 1984).

[15]See Michael Maccoby, *The Leader* (New York: Simon and Schuster, 1981) p. 219.

[16]See Bruce C. Birch and Larry L. Rasmussen, *Bible and Ethics in the Christian Life*, 2nd ed. (Minneapolis: Augsburg, 1989) pp. 189-202.

[17]William A. Cohen advances this sort of argument in *The Art of the Leader* (Englewood Cliffs, NJ: Prentice-Hall, 1990) pp. 71-78.

[18]Max De Pree, *Leadership Is An Art* (New York: Doubleday, 1989) p. 9.

[19]Robert D. Dale, *To Dream Again: How To Help Your Church Come Alive* (Nashville: Broadman, 1981) p. 36.

NAOMI'S JOURNEY

(RUTH 1:1-4:17)

Friends tried to prepare me for the shock.

"Surely she's not as bad as you say."

"Well, she's pretty bad. Don't expect too much."

Flowers in hand, I left the gift shop and climbed into the elevator. The walk from the nurse's desk to her room seemed miles long. Finally I knocked on a door at the end of a long dark hallway. What I saw inside totally unnerved me.

There she was, hunched over in the corner of the room like a piece of broken furniture. To be honest with you, I didn't even recognize her. Cold fluorescence carved deep valleys in her face, highlighting hollowed-out eye-sockets that made her look decades older than her years. Her once-black hair had all but fallen out from the chemotherapy. Only scattered wisps of fuzz protruded here and there from her bald scalp.

Leaning over to greet her, I had to hold my breath to keep from gagging. The very room exhaled the smell of death. What was left of Nancy—disciple of Jesus, deacon's wife, mother of two, Sunday School teacher—lay dying before me of brain cancer. Stricken down in her prime, all she could do was "groan and turn her face away" (Lam. 1:8).

Wordlessly she waited for me to say something, some greeting, some word of comfort. But nothing came out. I was too shocked by her appearance. Any word I might say seemed woefully inadequate. Eventually we lapsed into a few quiet words of conversation, but it was difficult. She talked about her disease, her family, her older sister from Chicago who'd flown in to watch the kids. She talked about the children in her Sunday School class. She talked about how much she missed her own bedroom, about how much she missed corporate worship, about how difficult it was becoming to pray.

Finally I said goodbye and left. Retreating down the hospital corridor, I found myself wondering whether I'd ever see her again. The drive home carried me back to the many times she had touched my life. Four years earlier I had helped her bury her cancer-ridden mother, an experience which in many ways she now had to go through all over again. Two years before that, I had watched her cry with her husband when he received his one and only pink slip and lost his job. It devastated him. Laid off with only six months to go before retirement, their world fell apart. He lost his job, his benefits, his pension and his self-respect, all in one afternoon.

Now she lay dying of cancer. I felt angry. It didn't seem fair that this family had to suffer so much while other families enjoyed their weekends at the Shore and their vacations in the Poconos. Carole Mayhall says it well:

> Do you know how I feel, Lord?
> Do you?
> I'm in a slimy pit.
> Mud.
> Mire.
> I claw at the walls.
> Scratch.
> Scream.
> I'm trying to hang on to Your promises
> In my heart I know there's a Rock beneath my feet
> Please, God,
> May my heart's knowledge of that Rock
> And the reality of feeling that Rock
> Become one and the same.
> Soon.[1]

Let me put it bluntly. I'm tired of watching people suffer. I used to think that ministry, especially ministry to the sick, would get easier to do over time. It doesn't, at least not for me. Hospital visits are still just as gut-wrenching. Funerals are still just as hard to preach. It hits especially hard when it's someone like Nancy. Nancy is a wonderful Christian woman. She's had to absorb one crushing blow after another in her life. Her faith is strong, but it's taking a beating. She still believes in God, but she's starting to wonder why.

To her tormented cry of "Why, God?," she seems to get no answer back. Only silence. Now she's beginning to wonder, with millions of people just like her, whether God cares anymore.

Watching her writhe in agony, all I could think to pray was "Why, Lord? Why such suffering? Why such pain?" Philip Yancey knows the feeling. In a recent study of the book of Job he reflects on three questions we sometimes want to ask God at moments like this. "God, are you being unfair? God, are you silent? God, are you hidden?"[2] These are tough questions. Every one of us who suffers—that is, every one of us—wrestles with questions like these at some point in our lives. Were we to be brutally honest with one another, we might even admit to those times when they pound on our hearts with an intense ferocity.

Nancy wants to say to God what Naomi says to the women of Bethlehem:

"Do not call me Naomi. Call me Mara. For Shadday has dealt very bitterly with me. I went away full, but Yahweh has brought me back empty" (Ruth 1:20).[3]

THE STORY

The story of Ruth is an endearing tale, a powerful little novella about love rediscovered and honor restored. Through a series of "chance" meetings, Boaz the Hebrew meets Ruth the Moabitess, a beautiful young woman who has fallen on hard times. When he finally recognizes, at midnight on a threshing floor of all places, that Ruth is interested in him, he comes to her rescue in classic heroic fashion. The couple marries, has a son, and "lives happily ever after."[4]

The "icing on the cake" comes when we discover at the end of the story who Boaz really is: the great-grandfather of David, Israel's quintessential king (Ruth 4:17). It's not hard to see why Israel loved this story.

But the book of Ruth is not some ancient Israelite equivalent to the Harlequin romance. This is no pulp fiction or escapist fantasy. Ruth is a hard, realistic look at the evils of famine, death, hardship, and prejudice. Like most biblical stories, this one can be approached from a variety of angles. We can read it solely as a

sentimental tale of romantic love, or we can read it boldly as a dynamic story about the power of faith.

Though the scribes responsible for preserving it called it Ruth, it could just as easily have been named for its other main character, Naomi. As proof, notice how the story is framed by statements about Naomi. At the beginning, Naomi is mentioned as the sole survivor of a family ravaged by tragedy. At the end, Naomi becomes the focus of the incident where the women of Bethlehem praise Naomi (not Ruth) for the child who's been born. (See Ruth 1:1-5; 4:14-15.)

Further, Naomi is the prime initiator of almost all the action which takes place here. She welcomes Ruth, a non-Hebrew, into her family, apparently without reservation. She takes Ruth home with her to Bethlehem. She encourages the all-important meeting with Boaz. After the marriage takes place, it is Naomi who serves as the nurse for the child, not Ruth, even though Ruth is the biological mother.

But most importantly, the central conflict in the story takes place entirely within Naomi. Naomi's faith is the faith most painfully challenged here, not Boaz's or Ruth's. Naomi is the character who suffers most. Naomi is the one who has to face the toughest questions, questions like:

> Should I leave Judah to follow my husband to Moab? Should I encourage my sons to marry non-Hebrew wives?[5] Should I return to Judah, or stay in Moab with my daughters-in-law? Should I try to take my Moabite daughters-in-law back with me to Judah, perhaps to a life cursed by ethnic hatred and religious prejudice?[6] Should I try to keep my husband's name alive?

The answer Naomi gives to these questions determines the shape of the narrative and the story of her life. This is one of the reasons why this story is such a timeless classic. All of us can identify with Naomi. All of us have asked or will ask at some point in our lives the same basic questions. Confronting conflicts like Naomi's is an inevitable consequence of the human experience.

Naomi's journey is our journey.

My friend Nancy has a lot in common with Naomi. Both are women of deep faith. Both are challenged by powerful forces to abandon that faith. Both are forced by desperate circumstances to make painful decisions under enormous stress.

There is, however, a major difference. On the surface, it seems minor, but in reality it reflects a profound distinction between opposing world views at the core of this story.

Naomi changes her name. This is the difference. Even in her deepest pain, Nancy would never think of doing such a thing, changing her name. Nancy is a postmodern Westerner. Naomi, however, is a premodern Oriental. Changing one's name today is unusual, at least in the West. Changing one's name in the ancient Near East, however, is not unusual.

Nor is it incidental to the plot of this story. In fact, biblical characters never change their names for frivolous reasons. There is always a reason, usually a critically important one. That's why it's important for us to ask why Naomi changes her name here.

At points of crisis, biblical characters sometimes change their names to indicate that they themselves have undergone a profound change. Name-changing signifies that something new has happened, something transformative and powerful. Jacob becomes Israel. Saul becomes Paul. Naomi becomes Mara. Name-changing is not an uncommon phenomenon in Scripture, but a time-honored custom deeply rooted in the Oriental world from which the Bible develops.[7]

Further, look at the particular name she chooses. The name "Naomi" means "pleasant." The name "Mara" means "bitter." By setting out the terms "Naomi" and "Mara" in Naomi's first speech, the narrator wants us to focus our attention on this change of identity. In fact, it sets the tone for the whole story.

The book of Ruth, therefore, is the story of one woman's journey from bitter to sweet, from brokenness to wholeness. By framing Naomi's life between the poles of "bitterness" and "sweetness," the book of Ruth becomes a voyage of discovery, a journey by which one woman's spiritual transformation becomes a model for others. Ultimately the narrator of this journey wants us to ask of Naomi a simple question:

"Will Mara ever become Naomi again?"

BITTERNESS

At first, we are told nothing of Naomi's initial pain: the pain of famine, the pain of leaving home, the pain of losing her husband, the excruciating pain of losing her children. These tragedies must have been incredibly hard to bear, yet practically nothing is said about them. Thus the book of Ruth begins a lot like the book of Job: quickly, economically, and unpretentiously. Within the space of five short verses the most devastating events in Naomi's life are telescoped into mere background material for the narrative which follows.

After things do get under way, Naomi's lament to the women of Bethlehem climaxes a whole series of complaints. Each complaint increases in intensity until the moment when Naomi dramatically changes her name. Speaking to her daughters-in-law, she makes the following seven statements in Ruth 1:8-21:

> "Go back to your mothers' houses."
> "Turn back, my daughters."
> "Why would you go with me?"
> "I am too old to help you."
> "Yahweh's hand has struck me."
> "Life is very bitter for me."

Finally, she says,

> "Call me Mara, not Naomi."

Thus when we first meet Naomi she is already a bitter woman, and, like most bitter people, needs to be handled with special care. Ruth provides this care with medicinal words which still minister to the weary and the depressed:

> Stop asking me to abandon you . . . .[8] I will go where you go, live where you live, worship whom you worship, and die where you die (Ruth 1:16-17).

Notice how Ruth ministers to her mother-in-law. She makes it clear that Naomi will not be allowed to badger or manipulate her. Yet she also makes it clear that she will never willingly abandon her to suffer alone. Ruth is a model of tender, firm ministry. Like all care-givers, she has to walk a tightrope between encouragement and admonition, between prophecy and pastoral care, and she does it very well—so well, in fact, that even the townspeople of Bethlehem notice:

Everything which you have done for your mother-in-law since her husband's death has been told me in detail: how you left your own father and mother, and your homeland, to come to a people you had never known before (Ruth 2:11).

Later at the threshing floor, Boaz adds: "It is publicly known that you are a woman of integrity" (Ruth 3:11).

ACCEPTANCE

The next time Naomi speaks, it is in response to a very basic human need: hunger. In fact, so hungry are these women that Ruth asks if she can go into the fields to glean for food behind the harvesters. This must have been a hard request for Naomi. Yes, begging in the fields is a privilege allotted to the poor in Israel (see Lev. 19:9-10), but Naomi is still a landowner, not one of the institutionalized poor (Ruth 4:3). Her problem is not that she has no land. Her problem is that she has no one left to work on her land. Every male in her family is dead, and all she has left is a widowed daughter-in-law, who isn't even a Hebrew.

She has to start all over again. From the bottom. From the beginning. After everything she's been through, it just doesn't seem fair. Naomi's problems look insurmountable. Thus, I read a profound sense of resignation in her voice when she says to Ruth:

"Go, my daughter" (Ruth 2:2).

How difficult it must have been for her to say these words. For with these words, Naomi is forced to admit that things haven't turned out the way she had planned. With these words, she has to admit that life can be hard, that hope can be terribly difficult to sustain.

Yet perhaps they also signify that Naomi has decided to accept her fate. She has decided to refuse all her other options. Nowhere does she suggest, for example, that Ruth simply go away and leave her alone. Nor does she suggest that the two of them madly run away together into some crazy fantasy world.[9] Nor does she sell out to a life of idleness and boredom.[10] All were options for women in the ancient world just as they are now.

I see few signs of denial here. Even though Naomi, the once-happy wife of Elimelek and respected mother of Mahlon and

Chilion, now finds herself forced by circumstances beyond her control to beg for food, she no longer complains to Yahweh. She no longer mourns for the dead. She no longer tries to drive Ruth away. She simply accepts the reality of her situation and tries to make the best of it.

HOPE

When Ruth returns from the fields that evening a number of significant changes have occurred. She has finally eaten what may have been her first real meal in a long time. She has made sure to bring home enough food to share with Naomi. And, oh yes ... she's met a man named Boaz.

Doubtless Naomi had a different kind of day. Looking out over the fields where her boys used to play, perhaps she reminisces about her life, about what life used to be like as a blushing bride and fawning mother. She sees the reminders of her former life; an unused plow, perhaps, or a broken piece of equipment left to rot in the Palestinian sun, and it takes her back to the good times she had with her husband and children. Bravely she fights back the horrid images of Moab which attack her incessantly, threatening to lock her forever into a prison of self-pity.

Finally the women meet and Naomi asks Ruth about her day. Ruth begins to share with her mother-in-law all the things which have happened to her.

Here the narrator teases us a bit. He has already told us that Boaz is a kinsman (Ruth 3:1). Yet Naomi still doesn't know who it is that Ruth has met . . . until she hears a name. Perhaps she hasn't heard it in a long time. Perhaps she hasn't heard it since she was a little girl.

Boaz. The man's name is Boaz.

Gone With the Wind is a powerful film. Ashley, the southern gentleman, has been away for years, fighting for the Confederacy in a losing cause. Melanie, his devoted bride, has been waiting patiently for his return. Long years of separation have taken their toll. Ashley experiences the agony of war and the loneliness of separation. Melanie has had to contend with hunger, sickness, Yankees, carpetbaggers, and more adolescent tantrums from Scarlet

O'Hara than anyone should have to suffer.

One day she looks up, and sees a faintly familiar figure in the distance. As the figure limps closer, she takes a second, closer look. Her eyes strain. Her heart beats faster. The figure nears the entrance to what once had been an elegant driveway. Her palms sweat with anticipation. Wordlessly she starts walking toward him. He starts limping toward her. Her walk breaks into a run. He throws away his cane.

Then it happens. They touch and kiss in a passionate embrace. It's Ashley! Ashley has finally come home from the war!

Hope. Everyone needs hope. Yet so few of us really know how to sustain it when things get tough. Naomi finds this hope when she suddenly realizes that Ruth has found a near-kinsman. Why? Because in ancient Israel, finding a near-kinsman to raise up children for the deceased means everything to a widow. The reason, again, has to do with the peculiarities of Oriental culture. According to the law of Moses, Israelite males are morally obligated to care for the widows of deceased kinsmen because Israelites considered it immoral to allow a kinsman's name to perish from the earth.

Finding Boaz, therefore, is supposed to be a happy ending to this story, not a sexist portrayal of a neurotic woman's dependence on a man for survival.[11] Boaz offers new hope because he's a *kinsman*, not just because he's a *man*.[12] His arrival in Naomi's life inspires her to dream of the day when Mara might become Naomi again. This hope permeates everything Naomi says and does through the end of the book. It affects not only the way she looks at her life, but ultimately at the way she looks at her God.

At the beginning of Ruth, Naomi is a bitter woman. Now, finding Boaz, something new, something truly redemptive happens. Her attitude changes. Her goals change. She dares to believe again that God might have a purpose for her life. She dares to plan again for a possible future. She dares to worship. In fact, the blessing she pronounces upon God when she hears the news about Boaz is the first hopeful statement about God in the entire book:

"May he (Boaz) be blessed by Yahweh, who has not abandoned his covenant loyalty to either the living or the dead" (Ruth 2:20).[13]

CONFLICT RESOLUTION

"Sandwich generation." That's what they're calling us. Overworked adults paying the bills for kids in college and parents in nursing homes at the same time.

The numbers are compelling. In 1900, only 4% of the U. S. was over 65 years of age. Today this figure is 12%, and projections for the year 2030 are as high as 22%. Further, the number of people over the age of 85 is growing dramatically. In 1940, there were only 365,000. In 1980, the figure was 2.2 million,[14] and some estimate that fully 1 out of 3 Americans will be considered elderly by the year 2025.[15]

Yet this does not mean that life is all that much better. Although people live longer than they used to, the quality of life among the elderly has not vastly improved. In fact, many elderly people suffer a greater number of chronic diseases now, over a longer period of time, than ever in history.

This means that, for a nation aging as rapidly as ours, the problem of chronic depression needs to be moved higher and higher up the agenda of ministry. I see it in the overcrowded hospitals and nursing homes I visit all the time. I believe the book of Ruth can be an indispensable resource for the "sandwich generation." We need all the help we can get.

Perhaps we will discover in Ruth many of the same issues with which our parents and grandparents wrestle. Adult daughters, especially, since the role of care-giver often falls hardest upon them, have a lot to gain from a study of Ruth. The burden of caring for an aging parent is great. Depression is common, particularly among the chronically ill. Ruth can help us carry this burden.[16]

Our generation is experiencing more role reversal—and to a greater degree—than any other generation before us. Adult children are painfully discovering every day how difficult it can be to care for an older, independent, sometimes cantankerous parent. In fact, it's sad to say it but it's true. Alongside the more common terminology of "child abuse," a new terminology is making its way into the common vernacular: "parent abuse." Parent abuse is becoming more and more common in our society:

Parentcare—unexpected, unplanned, unnatural—is bewildering

and oppressing to a multitude of middle-aged and younger adult children who are emotionally and financially unprepared to cope with this reversal of roles.[17]

Yet whether we apply Naomi's journey to our parents or our children, to our neighbors or ourselves, the message of this marvelous little book continues to minister—not just to the elderly, but to anyone who's suffered a serious loss. Naomi's journey from depression to hope could be *Mom's* journey, or *Dad's*. Ruth could be an effective, vital resource for helping the broken and depressed all around us find renewed hope.

All of us need to hear what Naomi hears.

All of us need to find a way out of our suffering.

All of us need to change our names.

QUESTIONS FOR DISCUSSION:

(1) What is the central conflict in the book of Ruth?

(2) Why does Naomi change her name?

(3) Without naming any names, do you know any "Maras"?

(4) Describe a bitter person you know who has overcome his/her bitterness. How did they do it?

(5) What role does faith play in overcoming bitterness?

(6) What role does Ruth play in Naomi's journey?

(7) What role does God play in our journeys?

ENDNOTES

[1]Carole Mayhall, *Help, Lord: My Whole Life Hurts* (Colorado Springs, CO: Navpress, 1988) pp. 64-65.

[2]Philip Yancey, *Disappointment With God: Three Questions No One Asks Aloud* (New York: Harper, 1988). Stanley Hauerwas reflects much the same way in his book *Naming the Silences: God, Medicine and the Problem of Suffering* (Grand Rapids: Eerdmans, 1990).

[3]For reflection about where Naomi may have developed this attitude toward Shadday (translated "Almighty" in the NRSV), see M. S. Moore, "Job's Texts of Terror," *The Catholic Biblical Quarterly* 55 (1993) pp. 662-675.

[4]Phyllis Trible states the theme clearly: "The story of Ruth and Naomi is a tale of human kindness and devotion transcending the limits of national- or self-interest. It is the book of the Old Testament which has long been cited as a perfect example of the art of telling a story." "Ruth, Book of," in *The Anchor Bible Dictionary*, vol. 5 (New York: Doubleday, 1992) p. 842.

[5]Marriage to foreigners was a deeply troubling question in ancient Israel. Contrast, for example, the diametrically opposed points of view in Jeremiah 29:6 and Nehemiah 13:23-27.

[6]Older scholarship argued that Ruth was written during the post-exilic period as a relatively progressive response to the problem of mixed marriages during the restoration (see Ezra 10; Nehemiah 13). More recent scholarship tries to date the book to the time of David or Solomon; Edward F. Campbell, *Ruth* (Anchor Bible 7; Garden City, NY: Doubleday, 1975).

[7]Even today, note how Eastern influence has played a major role in the name changes of people like Cassius Clay (Muhammad Ali), Lew Alcindor (Kareem Abdul-Jabbar), and Chris Jackson (Mahmoud Abdul-Raouf). In the West, most women still change their surnames when they marry, though this custom is now undergoing extensive change in some circles.

[8]Literally, "Stop pressuring me to abandon you."

[9]What we might call the "Thelma and Louise" approach to life—a reference to the 1991 film by Ridley Scott based on Callie Khouri's angry screenplay. Richard Schickel has a "politically correct" review in *Time* 137, 25 (June 24, 1991) pp. 52-56.

[10]Like Isaiah describes in Isaiah 32:9-12 and Amos describes in Amos 4:1-3.

[11]For further study, see Katherine Kersten, "How the Feminist Establishment Hurts Women," *Christianity Today* 38, 7 (June 20, 1994) pp. 20-25.

[12]See Deuteronomy 25:5-10. For further study, see M. S. Moore, *"Haggo'el*: The Cultural Gyroscope of Ancient Hebrew Society," *Restoration Quarterly* 23 (1980) 27-35.

[13]Katharine Sakenfeld offers a good study of "covenant loyalty" in her book *Faithfulness in Action* (Philadelphia: Fortress, 1985).

[14]Lissy Jarvik and Gary Small, *Parentcare: A Commonsense Guide for Adult Children* (New York: Crown, 1988) p. 2.

[15]James Halpern, *Helping Your Aging Parents* (New York: McGraw-Hill, 1987) p. 23.

[16]Eugenia Anderson-Ellis and Marsha Dryan have a great deal to say about the "feminization" of caretaking in *Aging Parents and You* (New York: Master Media Limited, 1988) pp. 11-13.

[17]Jarvik and Small, *Parentcare*, p. 6.

JOSEPH'S VICTORY

(GENESIS 37:2-45:15)

"Yep, it's broken, all right. . . . Two places. See? Here . . . and . . . here."

Bizarre. That's how it looked. Weird. I had never seen an X-ray of a real skull before. The only skulls I had ever seen were the kind that hang in department stores on Halloween. Looking at an X-ray of a friend's skull, plastered against that glowing screen in that eternally frozen grin they all seem to have—well, it felt a little strange, to say the least. Up close, those empty eyesockets look so lifeless and inert . . . .

The doctor's voice broke in.

"Would you like to see him now?"

Nodding silently, I went into the next room to talk to the face that matched the picture.

If anything, the face looked worse. Nose broken. Lip split. Eyes swollen. Welcoming me into the room, Jack tried to manage a smile, but what came over his face looked more like a sneer than a smile.

I asked, "What happened to you?"

He answered, "I guess I zigged when I should have zagged. . . ."

Ben and Sheila were two young college students who moved into our area to attend a local university. Neither were Christians or had much of a Christian background. Invited by a friend, they began attending our Thursday night Bible study on campus. This study met in a student's apartment and attracted people from a wide religious spectrum. Soon the two of them were coming to our college-age class at church, too. Both seemed eager to learn more about God and grow in the Word.

Sheila made friends easily. Friendly and willing to serve, she helped to teach, visit, cook, paint, drive, babysit, and do whatever else needed to be done. Someone new was always sitting next to Sheila, some seeker after truth, some pilgrim searching for God. Her spirit illuminated our lives like a candle in a dark room.

Ben, however, was another story. Terse and abrupt, he was exactly the opposite of Sheila. At first he seemed cordial enough. But soon he began disrupting classes with constant harangues about his pet peeves. He thrived on controversy, verbally assaulting anyone who dared disagree with him. He pestered people at all hours with phone calls and pouted whenever he didn't get his way. Ben was the "squeakiest wheel" in our fledgling campus ministry, the one always in need of the most "grease."

Sheila was dating him when they came to us, so she tried to explain his behavior to others. Soon she found herself having to excuse his outbursts. She found herself having to explain his idiosyncrasies. It wasn't long before she began to tire of Ben's childish behavior.

She tried to reason with him. She told him she wanted their relationship to aim toward a more spiritual plane. She wanted him to know that she cared for him, but she insisted that he stop treating her like his personal possession. As tactfully as she could, she tried to share the truth with Ben in love.

Ben never heard a word. In fact, her "little talks" (as he called them) made him angry and defensive. He couldn't understand why she wanted to "change things." He couldn't understand why she wouldn't let him monopolize her life. One minute he clung to her side like a wounded puppy, the next he bellowed at her like an embittered dictator. Perplexed by this, Sheila didn't know what to do. "How can a Christian act so insensitively?" she would ask. "Why won't he listen to me?"

As the weeks turned into months, Ben clamped down tighter and tighter on Sheila. He called her at her apartment constantly, just to check up on her. He overinvested completely in his relationship with her. I think he did this because early in his life Ben had decided, like so many others, that the best way to deal with loneliness is either to suppress it altogether or to overinvest in sexual relationships. Consequently Ben had no idea how to make friends with a male peer group, not to mention female. Thus, when he became a member of the church, he didn't understand what it meant to be "member" of anything.

Sheila suffered for months under his tyrannical clinging. Finally Jack, a leader in our campus ministry, couldn't stand it anymore. Jack was an older brother in the faith who had the gift of spiritual empathy. Genuinely concerned for both of them, he finally decided to go to Ben in the spirit of Matthew 18 and try to resolve the conflict.[1]

Face to face, rather than behind his back, Jack unveiled a number of carefully chosen concerns before Ben's guarded stare. Swallowing hard, he stepped out on faith, bravely asking Ben to reciprocate. He asked him about the surliness. He asked him about the neediness. He asked him about the sexism. He asked him about the loneliness.

He asked what he could do to help.

But again, Ben never heard a word. The Christian approach to conflict resolution had no effect whatsoever on this person. Rather than listen, rather than open up, rather than change his behavior, Ben told Jack to "mind his own business" and "stay out of my way." He rebuffed Jack's overtures toward reconciliation like a porcupine in a bad mood.

Things came to a head one Sunday night after church. Arriving at Sheila's apartment uninvited and unexpected, Ben exploded when Jack answered the door. Inflamed with anger he lunged through the door, viciously savaged Jack, and left him lying in a pool of blood. It was over in seconds. By the time Sheila made it downstairs to see what was the matter, Ben had already stormed off, leaving Jack semi-conscious on the floor.

She didn't know whether to call the police, drive Jack to the hospital or go after Ben herself.

Later, in the emergency room, as Sheila and I took a moment to sort things out, I finally discovered the whole sordid story. Never in my wildest dreams had I imagined something like this happening in our campus ministry. How could Christians, even young Christians, act like this? We had prayed so hard for so long for this ministry. How could a conflict like this reel so totally out of control?

THE STORY

We might put the same question to Jacob's family in the closing pages of Genesis. To ask it in Sheila's words, "How could Joseph's brothers be so insensitive? How could they conspire to murder their own flesh and blood?" And what about Joseph himself? How could he be so unaware of his brothers' feelings of inferiority?

The story of Joseph is the story of one lonely man's temptation to individualize his faith. It's a story about how hard it can be to love God *and* God's people at the same time. There are many ways to read this classic, of course, but perhaps none more relevant to the present age. Beset by a father who dotes on him, a pack of older brothers who hate him, and a foreign culture which isolates him from "home," Joseph is a survivor. And like all survivors, he weathers courageously the ordeals and challenges which drive many of us to utter despair. Whatever else it might teach us, the story of Joseph is a story about a courageous man who refuses to abandon his love for God or his love for God's people.

How in the world does he do it?

JOSEPH AND HIS FATHER

Reinhold Niebuhr was perhaps the most provocative theologian of our rapidly waning twentieth century. His father, Gustav, was a local minister in a conservative church—a German-speaking Pietist church to be exact. Devout and strict, Gustav appears to have been a rather temperamental man who played favorites among his three sons. Walter, the firstborn, reacted to this prejudice by choosing a career in journalism, against his father's wishes. Richard, the youngest, found it difficult to secure his father's love, and even after becoming a professor of theology at Yale Divinity School, spent years in personal agony searching for himself and the father's love he had always been denied.

Reinhold was the favorite. Gustav took him under his wing at a very early age, lavishing him with affection and unconditional love. He gave him that which he refused his other sons. In his memoirs, Reinhold credits this paternal attention with his decision to preach at an early age.

In fact, he remembers the exact moment when he and sixteen other teenagers recited a passage from Jeremiah under his father's approving gaze. Only later, in his retirement years, did he realize that the biblical passage he recited that day had a double meaning for Gustav:

"I have loved you with an everlasting love. Therefore I have continued my faithfulness to you" (Jer. 31:3).

Jeremiah used these words to express the unconditional love of God for Israel. Gustav chose them to express a twisted, conditional love for only one of his sons.[2]

Such was Jacob's treatment of Reuben, Simeon, Levi, Judah and the rest of his sons. To the end of their lives, Leah's children never received the same attention, the same love from their father that Rachel's children did. Joseph inherited a resentment that was generations old. Paternal prejudice is a powerful sub-theme coursing through all the patriarchal narratives of Genesis. Beginning with Abraham's treatment of his sons, then Isaac's treatment of his, Jacob's treatment of his sons is not at all out of the ordinary.[3]

Leah's sons have a whole list of reasons to hate him.

JOSEPH AND HIS BROTHERS

Against this background, Joseph tries hard to fit in, but he doesn't get very far. As the story opens, he "searches" for his brothers in more ways than one. During this "search" he unwittingly tramps, as adolescents often do, on the highly sensitized feelings of his insecure siblings. From the narrator's perspective, Joseph is a spontaneous, unpretentious, naive seventeen-year-old. He apparently has no idea how his brothers feel about him. Yet to Reuben and his brothers he is little more than a reminder of opportunities never extended and privileges never granted.

This hatred flares out of control when Joseph foolishly brings his father an "evil report" about the work of his brothers (Gen. 37:2). To speculate about the contents of this report is tempting, but futile. The phrase itself is used elsewhere to describe another famous "evil report," namely, the "evil report" of the ten spies in the wilderness in Numbers 12:20. But this tells us little. Whatever it is, when Reuben and his brothers find out what he's done, their rage starts to look for a way to retaliate against him.

Joseph then radicalizes this rage when he tries to tell them about his dreams—about their sheaves bowing down to his and their stars bowing to him. Obviously this teenager knows little about resentment and what it can do to insecure people like Reuben and Judah. Joseph sets himself up for retaliation and revenge without even realizing it.

The narrator highlights this by means of a rather chilling metaphor. The name "Joseph" literally means "the one added on," a fitting name for a baby brother. Joseph is the child "added on" to Jacob's already sizeable family (Gen. 30:24). But when Joseph shares his dreams with his brothers, the narrator uses the verbal root of this word to convey to us something of their intense hatred for him. After each dream, he describes their response as "adding more hatred upon him,"—an obvious pun on Joseph's name (see Gen. 37:5,8).

Brick by brick, therefore, Joseph's brothers keep "adding more hatred upon him" until their wall of protection becomes a fortress of malice. Eventually, no one can get inside. Not Joseph, not Jacob, not God, not anyone. Life inside this dungeon becomes twisted and petty, a place where the unthinkable becomes thinkable, the unspeakable speakable; a "pity party" where gossip and slander become as commonplace an occurrence as an afternoon talk show or a primetime mini-series.

Joseph's "search" runs terribly awry. Instead of "finding" his brothers—and the love he needs from his family—what he "finds" instead is a den of murderers. As soon as he walks into their lair, they slam the door, lock it tight and sell his soul to the highest bidder.

JOSEPH IN EGYPT

In autumn, 1931, Mohandas Gandhi arrived in London to a tumultuous welcome. England was preoccupied with several dilemmas at the time—a budget badly out of balance, a devalued currency, a textile industry woefully unemployed, a military establishment sullen and mutinous. Gandhi knew he would have a tough time fighting for India's needs against such a grim domestic agenda.

The British press had a field day with him. They scoffed at his piety and his manners. They ridiculed his dress, particularly his home-spun peasant loincloth. They asked him obscure, stupid questions about Indian religion and philosophy. They ridiculed his ideas about "passive resistance" and "universal brotherhood." They did everything they could to upset this soft-spoken, strange little man.

They also wondered at the same time what he planned to say to the mighty British empire.

Gandhi let them know soon enough. Attending the Round Table Conference on Indian affairs, he patiently waited his turn to speak while one stuffy diplomat after another droned on. Finally, his turn came. Rising to the podium, he wasted no time. Without notes or speaking aids of any kind, he quietly but firmly rebuked the royals, intellectuals and politicians in attendance for their blatant colonialist prejudices. He passionately pleaded for an independent India. He calmly listed all the advantages to England of Indian independence. He challenged his audience to seize the day and avoid bloodshed.

Many of those who were there that day were said to have remarked that Gandhi's speech was the most brilliant piece of oratory they had ever heard—and this from people who truly prized their ability to recognize a great speech.[4]

But he showed them more than mere eloquence. He also showed them intelligence. Noting England's mounting economic worries, he pinched the Empire at its most vulnerable spot.

> I said to myself while nearing the shores of this beautiful island of England: "Perchance it may be possible for you to convince the British ministers that India can be a valuable partner, not held by force, but by the silken cord of love. I thought that India might be of real assistance in balancing your budget."[5]

Joseph orchestrates a similar economic offense against the Pharaoh of Egypt. Whisked into Egypt a penniless Hebrew slave, he finds himself forced to spend years in obscurity and unjust imprisonment. When his moment comes to speak, however, he is prepared. He tells the Pharaoh what his dreams mean. He points his king toward a way out of his problems. He helps him figure out his economic future.

Like Gandhi, Joseph knows exactly how to handle a room full of beleaguered politicians.

Lest we overlook the obvious, however, we need to remember that Egypt is a long way from home for Joseph. Egypt is not Palestine. Egypt was an urban, polytheistic, powerful culture in Joseph's day. Yahweh worship was only one of many options available to Joseph. Monotheism itself was only one of many options. It must have been very difficult to maintain faith in Yahweh as the one true God. Compromise and coercion threatened compassion and integrity in his moral code. Assimilation to pagan religion, morals and ethics was a daily temptation for this Hebrew boy.[6]

On the surface, he seems to handle the pressure well. He goes from rags to riches in a remarkably short time, and the biblical narrator attributes this success solely to Yahweh. Yet we want to know what goes on under the surface. Taken at face value, this text can easily lead us to the conclusion that Joseph was somehow miraculously predestined to political greatness, even superhumanly shielded from all doubt during his life in Egypt.

In fact, this is precisely how the Jewish historian Artapanus saw him. To Artapanus, Joseph was a shrewd manager. According to him, Joseph was the "very first" ruler of Egypt to divide the land fairly and equitably among the rich and the poor. He invented a new standard of weights for Egypt. He became a land reformer as well as a "minister of finance." Artapanus even argues that Joseph probably engineered his own kidnapping because he knew that Egypt needed his help more than Palestine did.[7]

The biblical narrator is not so bold. The text itself refuses to speculate about Joseph like this. Predictably, Scripture never *directly* shows us Joseph's inner struggle, yet it does show us a few things *indirectly*, and I believe that this is not accidental. To be specific, the narrator mentions three details which taken together show us a great deal about Joseph's life.

First, we know that he marries the daughter of a pagan priest named Potiphera, a worshiper of Re, the sun-god (Gen. 41:45). Her name is Aseneth and the "romance" between them is conveyed to us through later Jewish legend.[8] The biblical text does not tell us what life was like as the son-in-law of a pagan priest, but we know that situations like this elsewhere in Scripture are usually painful and problematic.[9]

Second, we know that Joseph gives names to his children which are themselves quite revealing. (See Gen. 41:50-52.) "Manasseh" comes from a word which means "to forget," while "Ephraim" comes from a word which means "to be fruitful." The narrator tells us that Joseph chooses these names in thanksgiving to God for leading him safely out of prison. Yet note how each one of them is pregnant with irony. Later, when his brothers come before him, it becomes painfully clear that this man has in no way "forgotten" what happened to him at their hand. In fact, he still struggles with the "fruit" of their damaged sibling relationship.[10]

Third, we know that in addition to his ability to interpret dreams, Joseph becomes an expert in other kinds of divination during his sojourn in Egypt. In one of these he uses a "divining cup," probably to practice oil or water divination (Gen. 44:4-5, 15). Now, this is not the place to open up a detailed discussion of ancient Near Eastern divination, nor is this the place to list all the reasons why Israel eventually came to abhor it.[11] But we do want to point out that Joseph has become a professional diviner, a thoroughly magical practice in the ancient Near East.

Taken together, all of these details drive us to conclude that Joseph has become thoroughly Egyptianized, both socially and religiously, when his brothers show up for help at his door.

CONFLICT RESOLUTION

I believe the narrator mentions these details to us in order to explain why the eventual showdown between Joseph and his brothers is so painful. Now thoroughly Egyptianized, Joseph's conflict is an agonizing one. Should he reconcile himself to his Hebrew brothers? Or should he ignore their needs? Should he welcome them with open arms? Or should he give them what they immediately need (food) and send them packing?

Either path carries a degree of risk.

Either path begins a journey from which there can be no return.

He could just ignore them. Why dredge up the past? All of that was years ago. Joseph has a new life now. He has a good job, a pretty wife, two growing kids. Why risk it all now just to reconnect with a "family" that treated him like dirt? Sure, he misses his father and especially his brother Benjamin. . . .

But is reconciliation worth the risk?

Darrell Jodock says we have a difficult task before us. Like Joseph, many of us have been cut off from our roots. In addition, many of us have had bad experiences with the church. Many of us want to respond to Jesus, but frankly, we want nothing to do with His Body.

This attitude is firmly entrenched in contemporary Western culture today. Christians today are called by God to build Christian community among a people and a culture which is "no longer tied into an overarching framework of meaning about which there is community consensus."[12] Many of the people we meet every day, even those who make the effort to visit our church buildings, come from worlds very much like Joseph's—worlds where they've been hurt and abused, worlds where they've been abandoned and sold, worlds where they've been, in Jodock's words, "isolated and left to develop an individualized philosophy and set of values."[13]

Jodock is not alone in his assessment. *Secularized individualism* affects all major institutions of Western culture, whether we speak of marriage,[14] or the nature of religious authority,[15] or the interpretation of Scripture,[16] or the structural dynamics of the church itself.[17]

In other words, Joseph is a man on the edge. Joseph is a man who stands in real danger of abandoning his Hebrew heritage. Half of him feels that to reconcile with his brothers is to sanction injustice. The other half feels that to abandon his heritage is to abandon God. Like many of us, Joseph wants to believe in God, but he is sorely tempted to believe he can love God without loving God's people.

His temptation is real. And it's still with us.

All of us have a little of Joseph in us. Perhaps a brother or a sister has "sold you into captivity." Perhaps you've been lied to. Perhaps you've been through a marriage that hasn't worked out. Perhaps you've been through a vicious church split. Perhaps your parents have been cruel to you all your life. Perhaps you've been on the hurting side of any one of the conflicts mentioned above in this book.

Does this mean you will privatize your faith?

Does this mean you will renounce your commitment to the church?

Does this mean you will never become a minister of reconciliation?

Here's the bottom line. Reconciliation is impossible without forgiveness. Joseph knows this. Deep down in his bones, he believes this. That's why he lets his brothers back into his broken heart. That's why he forgives them. That's why he says:

> I am your brother Joseph whom you sold into Egypt. But do not be distressed or angry with yourselves because you sold me here. God sent me before you to preserve life. . . . It was not you who sent me here, but God (Gen. 45:4-8).[2]

Reconciliation is hard. If Joseph had given in to the temptation to become a pagan individualist, he would have lost his chance to come back to God—the God of his fathers, the God of the covenant. But you and I would have lost something, too. In a profound way each one of us would have lost one of our greatest heroes, one of our most stirring examples of what it means to persevere under pressure. Yes, Joseph is an example for us, all right, a "role model" in the true sense of the word—but not because he was never tempted. Joseph is our hero because he so powerfully *conquers* his temptation, and shows us how to conquer ours.

Like Joseph, we too have to decide what to do about our brothers and sisters, the church of the living God.

The point of this story is the plea of this book. Love cannot be Christian unless it is horizontal *and* vertical. One cannot be a believer in God *and* a spectator in the church. Reconciliation occurs only when there is repentance *and* confession. Leadership occurs only where there is vision *and* ethics. Parenting earns our kids' respect only when there is communication *and* discipline.

Like Joseph, we serve a God who prepares us for covenant by sending us faithful servants. We serve a God who engages us in covenant by allowing us to experience God's forgiveness through the sacrificial blood of Jesus Christ. We serve a God who sustains us in covenant through the powerful ministry of the Holy Spirit. We serve a God who calls us back to covenant by continuing to send us faithful servants—even when we don't recognize them, or welcome them, or particularly care to talk to them.

C. S. Lewis describes our only alternative in the words of the demon Screwtape:

> How they hated each other up there where the sun shone! How much more they hate each other now that they are forever conjoined, but not reconciled.[18]

QUESTIONS FOR DISCUSSION

(1) What is Ben's problem?
(2) Why do Joseph's brothers resent him?
(3) What is Joseph "searching" for?
(4) How is Jacob like Gustav Niebuhr?
(5) How is Joseph like Gandhi?
(6) What is Joseph's conflict?
(7) How does he resolve it?

ENDNOTES

[1]Matthew's great chapter on Christian forgiveness.

[2]See Richard W. Fox, *Reinhold Niebuhr: A Biography* (New York: Pantheon, 1985) pp. 6-14.

[3]For further study of this sub-theme, see Thomas W. Mann, *The Book of the Torah: The Narrative Integrity of the Pentateuch* (Atlanta: John Knox, 1988) pp. 51-52.

[4]According to sources cited by William Shirer, *Gandhi: A Memoir* (New York: Simon and Schuster, 1979) pp. 171-174.

[5]*Ibid.*, p. 170.

[6]A world, in other words, very much like ours, as James Thompson points out in *The Church in Exile: God's Counter Culture in a Non-Christian World* (Abilene: ACU Press, 1990) pp. vii-viii.

[7]Artapanus' history is preserved by the ancient church historian Eusebius in his work *Preparation for the Gospel*. Carl Holladay has an English translation in *Fragments from Hellenistic Jewish Authors: Volume I—Historians* (Chico, CA: Scholars Press, 1983) pp. 205-209.

[8]The legend of *Joseph and Aseneth* wrestles with the problem of Joseph's marriage to a pagan Egyptian. The author of this story explains the marriage as follows: Joseph only marries Aseneth *after* she destroys her idols and converts to monotheism. C. Burchard has a translation of this delightful tale in James Charlesworth, ed., *The Old Testament Pseudepigrapha*, vol. 2 (Garden City, NY: Doubleday, 1985) pp. 177-247.

[9]For example, Ahab's marriage to Jezebel in 1 Kings 16:31.

[10]Note also that in Genesis 41:45 Joseph himself accepts a pagan name, "Zapenath-paneah"—which is Egyptian for "the god speaks and he lives."

[11]I discuss this in detail in my dissertation *The Balaam Traditions: Their Character and Development* (Atlanta: Scholars Press, 1990) pp. 42-43.

[12]Darrell Jodock, *The Church's Bible: Its Contemporary Authority* (Minneapolis: Augsburg Fortress, 1989) p. 73.

[13]*Ibid.*

[14]Walter Kaspar, *Theology of Christian Marriage* (New York: Crossroad, 1989) pp. 10-11.

[15]Thomas Molnar, *The Pagan Temptation* (Grand Rapids: Eerdmans, 1987).

[16]See my review of LaGard Smith's well-meaning, but parochial study,

The Cultural Church: Winds of Change and the Call for a "New Herme-neutic" (Nashville: 20th Century Christian, 1992) in *Restoration Quarter-ly* 35 (1993) pp. 113-116.

[17]C. Leonard Allen, Richard T. Hughes and Michael R. Weed, *The Worldly Church: A Call for Biblical Renewal*, 2nd ed. (Abilene, TX: Abilene Christian University, 1991).

[18]C. S. Lewis, "Screwtape Proposes a Toast," in *The Screwtape Letters* (New York: Collier, 1982; first published in 1962) p. 171.

CHILDREN OF GOD

Children of God,
Washed in the blood,
Changed by the Spirit's endeavor,
Freed from the past,
Champions at last,
Bound by a love none can sever,
Master, Redeemer and Brother
Help us to love one another
Power to live,
Strength to forgive,
Grant to us now and forever.

Proud, angry words,
Meaningless words,
Always and only divide us
Who can receive
What we believe
If we cannot sing in chorus?
Master, Redeemer and Brother
Help us to love one another
Harmony clear
Help us to hear
When we allow you to sing us.

"Death on a Cross,"
"Suffered but loss"—
Words we sing over and over
Cannot bring life
When by our strife
We keep them hidden and covered
Master, Redeemer and Brother
Help us to love one another
Hearts that are sore,
Aching and poor
Yearn to awake and discover.

Children of God,
Washed in the blood,
Filled by the Spirit's endeavor
Tear down the sin
Blinding within
Grieving our Father and Maker
Master, Redeemer and Brother
Help us to love one another
Help us to claim
All in your name
Peace—when we treasure each other.

NAME AND AUTHOR INDEX